Springer Texts in Business and Economics

Springer Texts in Business and Economics (STBE) delivers high-quality instructional content for undergraduates and graduates in all areas of Business/Management Science and Economics. The series is comprised of self-contained books with a broad and comprehensive coverage that are suitable for class as well as for individual self-study. All texts are authored by established experts in their fields and offer a solid methodological background, often accompanied by problems and exercises.

Sibarata Das · Alexandros Mourmouras ·
Peter C. Rangazas

Study Guide for Economic Growth and Development

Springer

Sibarata Das
International Monetary Fund
Washington, DC, USA

Alexandros Mourmouras
International Monetary Fund
Washington, DC, USA

Peter C. Rangazas
Department of Economics
Indiana University-Indianapolis
Indianapolis, IN, USA

ISSN 2192-4333 ISSN 2192-4341 (electronic)
Springer Texts in Business and Economics
ISBN 978-3-031-57084-1 ISBN 978-3-031-57085-8 (eBook)
https://doi.org/10.1007/978-3-031-57085-8

© The Editor(s) (if applicable) and The Author(s), under exclusive license to Springer Nature Switzerland AG 2024

This work is subject to copyright. All rights are solely and exclusively licensed by the Publisher, whether the whole or part of the material is concerned, specifically the rights of translation, reprinting, reuse of illustrations, recitation, broadcasting, reproduction on microfilms or in any other physical way, and transmission or information storage and retrieval, electronic adaptation, computer software, or by similar or dissimilar methodology now known or hereafter developed.
The use of general descriptive names, registered names, trademarks, service marks, etc. in this publication does not imply, even in the absence of a specific statement, that such names are exempt from the relevant protective laws and regulations and therefore free for general use.
The publisher, the authors and the editors are safe to assume that the advice and information in this book are believed to be true and accurate at the date of publication. Neither the publisher nor the authors or the editors give a warranty, expressed or implied, with respect to the material contained herein or for any errors or omissions that may have been made. The publisher remains neutral with regard to jurisdictional claims in published maps and institutional affiliations.

This Springer imprint is published by the registered company Springer Nature Switzerland AG
The registered company address is: Gewerbestrasse 11, 6330 Cham, Switzerland

If disposing of this product, please recycle the paper.

Contents

Study Guide for Economic Growth and Development 1
   Overlapping-Generations Model of Economic Growth 3
   Fiscal Policy 29
   Schooling and Fertility 49
   A Complete One-Sector Model 65
   Two Sector Growth Models 81
   Wage and Fertility Gaps in Dual Economies 95
   Physical Capital in Dual Economies 107
   A Complete Dual Economy 119
   Urbanization 129
   Government Borrowing 141

Study Guide for Economic Growth and Development

Chapter 2
Overlapping-Generations Model of Economic Growth

Reader's Guide

Section 2.1   Firms and Production

Purpose: Link the productivity of labor and capital to the income that those inputs generate.

Sticking Points: (i) Where do the conditions for profit maximization, (2.2a) and (2.2b), come from? Economists derive the "best plans" for all economic agents by solving *mathematical optimization problems*. If you are curious about how this works, skim section A.2 of the Technical Appendix at the end of the book

(ii) More importantly, you need to understand the rules for profit-maximization at an intuitive level. It may help to relate the discussion in the text back to your microeconomics principles course. To do this, studying Question 3 and its solution will be helpful.

Take Away: Accumulating physical capital per worker (k) makes workers more productive and increases their wages—the primary source of a household's living standard.

Section 2.2   Households

Purpose: Show how household savings provides the physical capital available for firms to use in production.

Sticking Points   (i) In actual economies, most households save by buying financial assets such as stocks, bonds, and bank accounts (although in many developing economies these assets do not exist and households are forced to save by purchasing physical capital directly). These financial assets are just claims on physical capital. For simplicity, we bypass the financial middle-men (intermediaries such as banks and brokers) that issue financial assets and assume that households purchase physical capital directly.

(ii) There is a subtle timing issue that has an important implication. Households save and accumulate capital over their working lives and then rent the capital out to firms during retirement to finance their consumption in old age. This means, in any period, the number of capital *owners* (last period's workers or this period's retirees) may be different than the number of workers that *use* the capital in production. If the population is growing fast (n is high), then it becomes difficult for the economy to raise capital per worker (k).

(iii) Where do the optimal consumption and saving equations (2.5a, 2.5b, and 2.5c) come from? Same answer as for the profit maximizing equations of the firm in section 2.1. We assume that households, just as with firms, are trying to do the best they can when making choices. This means we can find the behavioral implications by solving a mathematical optimization problem where households choose their plans to maximize lifetime utility subject to a budget constraint. The details are in the Technical Appendix but you primarily need to grasp the basic intuition as revealed in questions such as Question 7.

Take-Away: The supply of physical capital in an economy is determined by household savings which is a fraction of lifetime wage income.

Section 2.3 Competitive Equilibrium

Purpose: To explore the underlying dynamics of the economy that leads to growth and development.

Sticking Points: (i) To understand economic growth, you need to go beyond the standard one period snapshot of a static equilibrium (see Fig 2.1). We have to dig deeper into the capital market equilibrium condition that says the capital-labor ratio this period was determined by the saving plans of workers last period: $k_t = \frac{\beta}{1+\beta} \frac{w_{t-1}}{n} = \frac{\beta}{1+\beta} \frac{(1-\alpha)Ak_{t-1}^\alpha}{n}$. It is the fact that last period's capital-labor ratio determines wages, a portion of which is saved, that makes a dynamic connection: $k_{t-1} \rightarrow k_t$ or in words: previous period's capital → worker productivity→ wages → retirement saving → this period's capital.

(ii) The diagram (Fig 2.2) that sketches the dynamic relationship given by the transition equation (2.8) is the foundation of much of the modeling that follows in the course. You need to understand Fig. 2.2 completely.

Take-Away implications. The transition equation exhibited in Fig 2.2 reveals three important

(i) An economy's growth is relatively rapid when it is far from its long-run potential (steady state)

(ii) An economy's growth rate slows as it builds up capital or "industrializes."

(iii) Growth will stop when the economy reaches the highest capital-labor ratio it can maintain.

Sections 2.3.1-2.3.2   *Growth Analytics*

Purpose: To develop the analytical skills needed to use the transition equation and Fig 2.2, just as you did with the demand and supply models of introductory economics.

Sticking Points   Sections 2.3.1 and 2.3.2 are crucial for understanding how the growth process is altered by various events. We have seen how the sketch of the transition equation can depict economic growth through the accumulation of private capital. The sketch can also be used to analyze how various events impact the growth process. There are two general categories of such events: *changes in the fundamental structure* of economies, as captured by the parameters β, A, and n, and *discrete shocks* to the values of K and N due to events not captured by the gradual growth process. It is important to see how each category of events affects economic growth in the short-run and the long-run.

Take-Away   The results of the growth analytics can be summarized as follows. Be able to explain the effects of each type of shock.

	Effect on Worker Productivity			
Positive Shock in	Level		Growth rate	
	Short-run	Long-run	Short-run	Long-run
β	higher (period after shock)	higher	higher	no effect
A	higher	higher	higher	no effect
n	lower (period after shock)	lower	lower	no effect
K	higher	no effect	higher then negative	no effect
N	lower	no effect	lower then positive	no effect

Section 2.3.3 Technical Progress

Purpose: The current version of the model predicts that economic growth will converge to zero. We have had positive economic growth for over two centuries—too long for the prediction to be plausible. *Technical knowledge*—new ideas about production and machine design must be added to allow for long-run steady state growth.

Sticking Points (i) Our modeling of technical progress is based on the concept called the *efficient labor input* (H) which adjusts the actual work force (M) with an index that captures how technology makes a given worker more productive (D).

(ii) With the new concept of labor input, we can proceed just as before if we redefine k as the ratio of physical capital to the effective workforce. This new definition reveals one drawback of technical progress—as new ideas and types of machines make workers more productive, an economy will find it more difficult to supply workers with the needed quantity of capital.

(iii) Technical progress alters how the growth rate in worker productivity evolves. Pay special attention to the last two equations in this section.

Take-Away: We now have two sources of economic growth: a transitory *endogenous* source that we can fully explain (k) and a permanent *exogenous* source that is not explained within the model (D).

Section 2.4 Testing the Model

Purpose: With the addition of technical progress, the model seems to yield reasonable predictions. But just how accurate are the predictions when compared to real world data? And how much growth can be explained by the endogenous component, physical capital accumulation? This section answers these questions by using the model in an attempt to replicate historical growth in the US.

Sticking Points: (i) The model is calibrated to generate the observed growth of worker productivity in the US from 1870 to 1990. So what's the test if the simulation is rigged to capture the total growth over the period? The test is to see if the model predicts the correct *pattern* of growth rates and interest rates over time. Both growth rates and interest rates showed little trend during most of the 20th century.

(ii) Problem 19 gives the details of how the simulation is constructed. Jumping right into Problem 19 might be a bit much. Problem 18 eases you into how the simulation is done.

Take-Away: The model misses the mark on the pattern of growth rates and interest rates—the model predicts that they both should have declined much more than they did over the historical period. The main conclusion is that physical capital accumulation per worker can only explain a relatively small part of historical growth.

Section 2.5   Human Capital

Purpose: The historical simulation revealed that sources other than physical capital must have contributed to economic growth. In this section we assess whether public education could have significantly increased worker productivity, while maintaining consistency with the data.

Sticking Points   (i) A new modeling adjustment generalizes the concept of effective labor supply using equation (2.15) which now includes the effects of student time and resources devoted to public education. Notice that if public education investments do not raise worker productivity then $\theta_1 = \theta_2 = 0$ and the effective labor input is solely determined by the technology index as we assumed previously.

(ii) We can rewrite (2.15) as $H_t = D_t M_t h_t$, with $h_t = (x_{t-1}/D_t)^{\theta_1} e_{t-1}^{\theta_2}$ as the new modeling component that picks up the effect of public education on worker productivity. Equipped with estimates of θ_1 and θ_2, along with the data on public school investments given in Table 2.2, we can redo the historical simulation in the same fashion as before but now with three sources of growth (k_t, h_t, D_t).

Take-Away   When we attempt to explain half of the historical growth with the contribution of both k_t and h_t, the predictions of the model match the trendless growth rates and interest rates observed over the 20th century. We now have a good explanation for half of the historical growth in the US. Other growth investments are added in Chapter 3 to make further progress. Later in the text, we identify gains in worker productivity that result from improved efficiency in the allocation of resources.

2.6   Intergenerational Transfers

Purpose: A theory of human capital accumulation naturally begins with parents that have a preference to improve the life-chances of their children by investing in their skills.

Sticking Points: (i) The altruistic motive for investing in children leads to a rather complex formulation of household behavior. It allows one to go from an overlapping generations model to an infinitely-lived agent model, linking the two workhorse models of macroeconomics. The infinitely-lived agent model has advantages (see Appendix B of this chapter) and one must at least be familiar with it to read the macroeconomics literature. However, for our purposes it is not essential.

(ii) The 'warm-glow" approach to modeling a preference for intergenerational transfers is simpler than the altruism approach and in some ways is more empirically accurate. It is the approach we use when modeling transfers.

Take-Away: Intergenerational transfers are important for economic growth and macroeconomics in general. For our purposes, using the warm glow motivation for transfers suffices.

Solutions to Exercises

Questions

1.   (a) *Technology* generally refers to disembodied ideas about production. In practice, it has two meanings. First, it refers to the entire production function, such as the Cobb-Douglas production function given in (2.1). The production function is a mathematical representation of how production takes place and what inputs are needed. Second, a narrow use of the word focuses directly on how the productivity of labor, via the technology index (D), changes over time as new ideas are discovered and developed. The productivity index is introduced in section 2.3.
   More concretely one can think of technology as a collection of ideas about production methods and organization of the firm, machine design that improves function, exogenous aspects of the skills and health of the workforce, and complementary inputs that may not be explicitly modeled (such as seeds, fertilizer, energy inputs, and public infrastructure)
   (b), (c), (d) *Capital* refers to the assets used in production. Capital is comprised of physical and human capital. *Physical capital* refers to physical assets such as plant and equipment and, in some applications, land. *Human Capital* refers to the stock of embodied knowledge and skills possessed by the work force that are explicitly modeled. If human capital is not explicitly modeled, then its contribution to production is contained in the productivity index, D.

2.   Equations (2.2a) and (2.2b) are conditions that must be satisfied for the firm to be maximizing profit in a competitive market setting where the factor prices are taken as given. The equations say that the marginal benefit of choosing the inputs, represented by the marginal products, is equal to the marginal cost of choosing the inputs, represented by the factor prices.
   A tricky feature of these equations is that they seem to give two equations that the capital-labor ratio must satisfy. For given factor prices, the two resulting solutions for the capital-labor ratio will not generally be consistent. So, one cannot think of these equations as being satisfied at the level of the firm for *any* factor prices. Instead, one of the equations must be thought of as determining one of the equilibrium factor prices (w or r). The other factor price will be determined by the condition that the demand for the capital-labor ratio must equal the supply of capital relative to labor supplied by the households. It is intuitive to think of w and k

as determined by (2.2a) and (2.2b), with the price of capital, r, determined by a market-clearing condition for the capital market.

3. The marginal product of labor is a downward-sloping function of the employment level, for a given capital stock, due to diminishing marginal productivity. The competitive market wage is not affected by the employment choice of an individual firm. It is represented by a horizontal line. The profit-maximizing employment choice is found where the wage rate and the marginal product curve intersects, indicating that (2.2b) is satisfied.

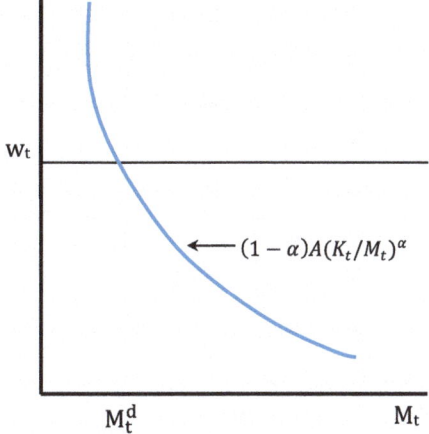

A larger capital stock shifts the marginal product curve upward. For a given wage rate, this would lead to an increase in the firm's demand for labor, as the profit-maximizing intersection shifts to the right. An increase in A does the same. If the market wage increases the quantity of labor demanded decreases (a movement along the labor demand curve).

4. The average product is $\dfrac{Y_t}{M_t} \equiv y_t = A k_t^\alpha$ and the marginal product is $\dfrac{\Delta Y_t}{\Delta M_t} = (1-\alpha) A k_t^\alpha$.

The two concepts are proportional to each other with the marginal product being smaller by the constant factor $1-\alpha$. The average product is the observable measure of worker productivity. In theory, the marginal product informs the firm about hiring additional workers. As long as the marginal product exceeds the market wage, it makes sense for a firm to hire another worker. For this reason, profit maximization requires that workers be hired until the marginal product is equal to the wage rate.

5. The capital and labor shares are the fractions of total income paid to owners of capital and to workers. With a Cobb-Douglas production function the income shares are the constants α and $1-\alpha$, respectively. Until very recently the evidence supported the prediction of constant income shares with the capital share being approximately 1/3 and the labor share being

approximately 2/3. However, since the turn of the last century, it appears that the capital share has been rising and the labor share has been falling. The changes appear to have ended around 2010, when the shares again remained constant but at new levels. Economists do not yet have a conclusive explanation for this surprising change.

6. The *rental rate* on physical capital is the payment that the firm makes to the capital owner for renting one unit of capital that is used in production. The rental rate is denoted by r. The *rate of return* on capital is the rental rate received by the owner minus the depreciation rate, that part of the capital that is lost in production. The rate of return is then $r - \delta$. The interest rate is the rate of return on financial assets. If financial assets exist and are held in equilibrium, the interest rate must equal the return on physical assets. So, the interest rate must also equal $r - \delta$. In most of the analysis of this book, we abstract from any financial assets. Nevertheless, it is common for economists to refer to $r - \delta$ as the "interest rate."

7. (a) A higher wage raises current and future consumption (both are "normal" goods with positive income effects under our assumptions). An increase in future consumption when the wage is higher requires an increase in saving.

(b) In general, the return to capital has an ambiguous effect on current consumption because of conflicting *income* and *substitution* effects. Households rent capital, so a higher return raises lifetime resources, allowing households to afford more consumption in each period of life. However, a higher return also raises the cost of current consumption because every unit of current consumption now means more units of future consumption are forgone. The increased cost causes households to substitute away from the relatively more expensive current consumption in favor of the relatively cheaper future consumption. The strengths of these opposing effects on current consumption are determined by the intertemporal elasticity of substitution, σ (see *Problem* 7). The higher is σ, the greater is the willingness to substitute consumption across time and the more likely it is that the substitution effect dominates the income effect. With $\sigma = 1$, which corresponds to our standard log preferences, these two effects exactly cancel. So there is no effect of the return to capital on current consumption and saving. However, a higher return to capital will increase future consumption because the income and substitution effects are reinforcing in this case.

(c) A higher value of β means households are more patient. Greater patience lowers the value of current consumption relative to future consumption. Thus, current consumption falls in favor of more saving and future consumption.

8. The interest elasticity of saving measures the response of saving to changes in the interest rate. Technically, it is the percentage change in saving divided by the percentage change in the interest rate. Economic theory predicts an ambiguous interest elasticity because of conflicting substitution and income effects—see *Questions* 7 and 9 and *Problems* 6 and 7. For the preferences assumed in the text, the elasticity is zero because the two conceptual effects exactly cancel. This is roughly consistent with the very low empirical measures of the interest elasticity typically estimated in the literature.

9. First, an explanation for the *slope* of the supply of capital. Equation (7) gives the supply of capital that is financed by last period's saving. How saving is related to the interest rate depends on the value of the parameter σ (see *Question* 7 and *Problem* 7). The ambiguous effect of the interest rate on saving is because of two opposing effects. The *substitution effect* says when the interest rate increases, current consumption is relatively more expensive in present value than is future consumption— causing a substitution of less current consumption for more future consumption. This effect causes current consumption to fall and saving to increase with the interest rate. The *income or wealth effect* says that when the interest rate increases all savers (which all young households are in this model) have greater future income or wealth because at any level of saving there is more interest income in the second period. The greater income causes households to increase their demand for current and future consumption, causing saving to fall. Thus, the income effect causes current consumption to increase and saving to fall as the interest rate increases.

The relative strength of the substitution and income effects is determined by the parameter σ. The higher is σ the stronger is the substitution effect and the weaker is the income effect. When σ exceeds one, higher interest rates cause more saving. In this case, the supply of capital has a positive slope. When σ equals one, higher interest rates cause exactly offsetting substitution and income effects, resulting in no change in saving. In this case, the supply of capital matches the sketch of (2.7) in the Figure, a perfectly vertical line because the level of saving is independent of the interest rate. Finally, when σ is less than one, the supply of capital is downward sloping because higher interest rates cause less saving.

The values of w and n cause the sketch of (2.7) to "shift." An increase in w_{t-1} causes an increase in saving, and next period's supply of capital, for every possible interest rate. This is displayed as a rightward shift in the capital supply curve.

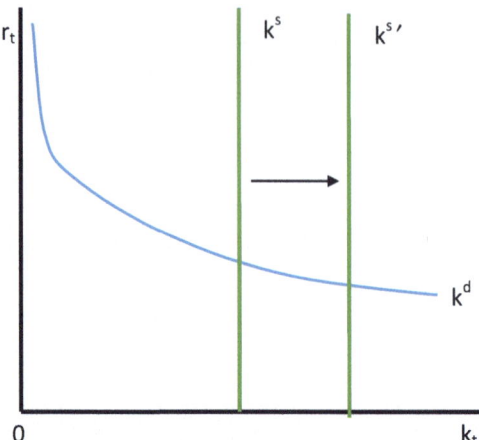

An increase in *n* lowers the capital per worker at every given interest rate, resulting in a leftward shift in the capital supply curve. This negative effect from population growth is explained intuitively in *Question 17*.

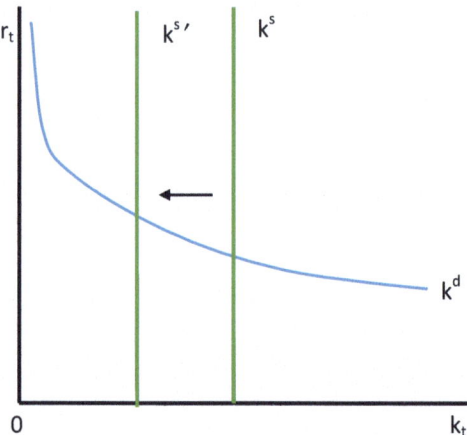

10. The transition equation comes directly from the capital market equilibrium condition that states the capital available to workers in the next period equals the capital accumulated for retirement saving by the current period workforce. The right-hand-side of the transition equation

simply represents current period saving expressed as a function of the current capital-labor ratio that determines the wage rate.

11. A higher capital-labor ratio this period causes a higher wage. A higher wage increases saving and the supply of capital for next period. The linkage becomes weaker because the effect of the capital-labor ratio on wages is subject to diminishing returns. Each increment in the capital-labor ratio results in a smaller increase in wages and saving and thus a smaller increase in next period's capital-labor ratio.

12. When the economy starts below the steady state, capital is accumulated. However, for the reason outlined in *Question* 11, the increase in the capital stock in each period becomes smaller causing the growth rate to slow.

When the economy starts above the steady state, the capital-labor ratio shrinks. This happens because the wage and resulting saving at the current capital-labor ratio is too small to finance a new capital-labor ratio that is as large as the existing one. This causes the new capital-labor ratio in each period to be smaller than in the previous period, creating a negative growth rate. The absolute value of the negative growth rate becomes smaller each period as the economy tracks to the steady state from above. So, the growth rate increases (a smaller negative growth rate each period).

13. (a) worker productivity rises with the capital-labor ratio

(b) the growth rate of worker productivity, while positive during the transition to the steady state, becomes smaller as the effect of the capital-labor ratio weakens

(c) wages equal the marginal product of labor, so they also rise during the transition

(d) the return to capital equals the marginal product of capital, so both fall as the capital-labor ratio increases due to diminishing marginal productivity

14. (a) An increase in total factor productivity (TFP or A) raises current wages for any given value of the current period capital-labor ratio. Thus, households will save more, at the same saving rate, causing the future capital-labor ratio to be higher (an upward shift in the transition equation)

(b) An increase in the saving rate (due to a higher value of β) means more of the current wage is saved to accumulate capital for retirement, causing the future capital-labor ratio to be higher (an upward shift in the transition equation)

(c) An increase in the population growth rate (due to a higher value of n) means there will be more workers in the next period relative to those saving this period, causing the available capital in the future to be spread more thinly across the relatively larger future workforce (a downward shift in the transition equation)

(d) A permanent one-time jump in the economy's population size will decrease the capital stock available to each member of the new larger workforce in the *current* period, causing the current capital-labor ratio to move leftward down along the horizontal axis closer to the origin. This causes the economy to resume its transition to the same steady state along the same transition equation but starting from a position farther away from the steady state. The transition equation does not shift because the increase in population size affects the current population and the future population by the same amount, so the rate of population growth (n) between current and future period remains the same.

(e) A natural disaster that destroys some of the existing capital stock will lower the capital-labor ratio in the current period, causing the current capital-labor ratio to move leftward down along the horizontal axis closer to the origin. The event does not alter any of the fundamental parameters that determine the position of the transition equation, so transition equation does not shift.

15. If the two economies have the same structure, they have the same transition equation for the capital-labor ratio and the same steady state. Economy A has the higher capital-labor ratio and the higher wage. Although, the interest rate is lower in A, we always assume that the standard of living is higher when the wage rate is higher (this is the most relevant case but not the only possibility—growth can be bad if a country accumulates "too much" capital!). However, since A is closer to the steady state, it will grow slower. Thus, over time, B will catch up or converge to A in in terms of the capital-labor ratio, wages, and standard of living.

This type of convergence will not happen if the structures of the two economies are different. Country B might be poor not only because it is undeveloped, in the sense of having low initial k. It may be more fundamentally poor because its value of TFP is low or its population growth rate is high. In this case the poor country's transition equation and steady state is strictly below that of country A, and convergence is not possible. So, poor countries will not *unconditionally converge* to rich countries, the convergence is *conditional* on the countries having the same structure, i.e. the same transition equation.

The model's prediction about convergence is borne out in the data. The average growth rate among poor countries is about the same as the growth rate in rich countries, so in general poor countries do *not* converge to the worker productivity and living standards of rich countries. Only those poor countries with similar transition equations as rich countries experience convergence.

16. As the model predicts, there is evidence of a slowdown in growth rates as economies become more developed. The slowdown has only become clear recently because long-term trends are hard to identify. See Chapters 3, 9, and especially 11 for more discussion. However, it does not appear that growth stops altogether. Most economists feel that it is reasonable to assume a positive steady state growth rate that results from ongoing new ideas about production—i.e. technological progress. The plausibility of this assumption is discussed in Chapters 3 and 11.

17. We have seen in *Questions* 9 and 14 that a higher population growth rate reduces the supply of capital per worker. This happens because the saving that generates the supply of capital is provided by one generation of workers and the workers that use the capital are from the next generation. A high population growth means that the number of workers that use the capital

in production next period will be high compared to the number of workers that provide the saving this period. The saving of the current generation of workers is thus "diluted" or spread over more future workers, lowering the capital-labor ratio. Note that this has nothing to do with the *absolute* size of the population (more households mean both more savers and more workers) but rather with the supply of savers *relative* to the supply of future workers, which depends on the population growth rate.

A high population growth rate then lowers the capital-labor ratio, the wage, and the standard of living of a country.

18. From (9) we can see that population growth and technological progress enter the transition equation symmetrically. This is because both cause the effective labor supply to grow over time—population growth increases the actual number of workers and technological change increases a given worker's productivity, making the effective work force higher. An increase in either lowers the capital stock relative to the effective labor supply, which lowers the wage per unit of effective labor supply and raises the interest rate. The difference between the two sources of growth in the effective labor supply is that while population growth lowers labor productivity per actual worker, technological progress raises labor productivity per actual worker (the direct positive effect of technology more than offsets the indirect negative effect of lower capital intensity).

19. (a) Using the compounding formula, $(1+d^a)^{30} = 1.01^{30} = 1.3478 = 1+d$, so $d = 0.3478$.

(b) In the steady state, we have $\dfrac{Y_t}{M_t} = \dfrac{A\bar{k}^\alpha D_t M_t}{M_t} = A\bar{k}^\alpha D_t$ (see also *Problem 16*). So,

worker productivity will grow at the same rate as D, 1 percent on an annual basis.

(c) An economy that is below the steady state will grow faster than 1 percent per year because there will be additional growth through increases in k.

20. Calibration is a form of estimation—the setting of parameters and initial conditions of a model to numerical values. The purpose of calibration is to generate quantitative predictions about the model's endogenous variables. The predictions can be used to check the economic importance of certain mechanisms in the model and to assess the empirical relevance of the model by comparing the model's predictions to available data.

The basic growth model of this chapter was calibrated to match statistical estimates of the parameters, when available. Other parameters were set to match certain target values for some of the endogenous variables. The model was then tested by comparing simulated growth paths to historical growth paths in the U.S.

21. The initial capital-labor ratio of the calibrated model was set to generate half the actual growth in U.S. worker productivity from 1870 to 1990 (the other half is generated by exogenous technical progress). The model was unable to capture key features of U.S. growth—in particular, the trendless growth rates in worker productivity and interest rates over the 20th century. This

failure stems from the fact that the basic neoclassical model of physical capital accumulation predicts declining growth rates and interest rates.

22. Human capital is the set of skills and ability embodied in a worker. In our model, human capital is generated from formal education. The two key inputs in the human capital production function are student time and inputs provided by schools. The U.S. historical data on each input is provided in Table 2.2.

To add human capital to our calibration exercise, we use the data from Table 2 to first compute $\tilde{x}_4 / \tilde{x}_0 = (9.5 / D_5) / (1 / D_1) = 9.5 / (1+d)^4 = 3.6656$. Next, compute

$$\frac{h_5}{h_1} = \left(\frac{\tilde{x}_4}{\tilde{x}_0}\right)^{\theta_1} \left(\frac{e_4}{e_0}\right)^{\theta_2} = (3.6656)^{0.10} \left(\frac{0.29}{0.08}\right)^{0.40} = 1.9061.$$ Greater schooling inputs caused average worker skills and productivity to almost double from 1870 to 1990.

23. We introduced human capital in the model as resulting from *exogenous* investments in public education. The investments included actual estimates of student time and school expenditures in the U.S. over the 1870 to 1990 period. We used a human capital production calibrated in previous work and added it to the neoclassical growth model of physical capital accumulation. We once again attempted to explain half of the observed growth over the period, with the remaining half explained by exogenous technological progress. The difference between this experiment and the experiment using the basic neoclassical growth model is that we no longer need to rely heavily on physical capital accumulation to explain growth.

The results were promising in that the simulated growth path exhibited little downward trend in growth and interest rates. This was possible for two reasons. First, the initial capital-labor ratio could be set much closer to its steady state value. Second, while human capital accumulation is also subject to diminishing returns, the investments in human capital rose quickly enough to offset the diminishing returns and keep the growth rates relatively constant. The trick is now to develop a theory of *endogenous* human capital investments that can reproduce this outcome.

24. A human capital transfer is an investment of parent's time to create knowledge or skills in their young children or a payment for goods that help the child learn such as books, computers, or professional teaching services. Financial transfers are income transfers that the child can use to purchase any good or service when they are adults. A payment of college tuition is equivalent to a financial transfer if the child is (i) financially independent and (ii) at least investing as much as the amount of the financial transfers herself (financed by her own wages or a college loan). In this case, the child can simply withhold the amount of the parents' tuition payment from their own contribution and use it to buy *any* goods and services they desire. College loans do not help alleviate the lack of family funds during the years that the child is dependent. If human capital investment and schooling are low in these early years, it affects the chances of the child developing enough human capital to attend or succeed at the college level.

25. Under altruism, the parent attempts to maximize the lifetime wealth of their children. With sufficient resources and altruistic concern, the parent achieves this by investing in human capital up to the point where the return on the last unit of investment yields an increase in earnings that is equal to the return of saving that unit of income in financial or physical assets. After this point, the child's wealth is maximized by leaving them financial or physical assets that yield the market interest rate, which is a greater return than further investment in human capital. If resources and altruistic concern are not sufficient to make human capital investments large enough to drive the return down to the market interest rate, then no financial or physical assets will be transferred. In this case the marginal return on human capital investment will be above the market interest rate. This is not productively efficient because less investment in physical assets and more investment in human capital would raise future income.

26. As suggested in the hint, when there are unconstrained intergenerational transfers, the economics determining the timing of consumption *within an individual's life* is analogous to the economics determining the timing of consumption *across different generations* of the family. The logic of how the interest rate affects the timing of life-cycle consumption, applies to the timing of consumption across generations. A higher interest rate will cause future consumption to rise relative to current consumption. In both cases the change in current consumption can be positive, zero, or negative, depending on the strength of substitution and income effects associated with the change in the interest rate.

If the household is constrained, the strict analogy made above no longer applies because financial assets cannot be used to determine the timing of consumption across generations, as only human capital transfers are being made. However, the logic is still very close. An increase in w_{t+1} raises the return to human capital investments. Just as with an increase in the interest rate, this will cause the next generation's consumption to rise relative to the current generation's. And, just as with an increase in the interest rate, the effect on current consumption and human capital investment is ambiguous because of opposing income and substitution effects. The higher value of w_{t+1} implies that family resources are higher because of a rise in the future generation's earnings. The parent can also benefit from the rise in the future generation's earnings by investing less in the child and consuming more. On the other hand, the future generation's consumption has become cheaper relative to the parents' consumption because the opportunity cost of not investing in human capital has gone up. This creates a substitution effect toward investment and away from consumption. Thus, the overall effect is ambiguous.

27. As explained in *Question* 26, an increase in w_{t+1} has an ambiguous effect on human capital investment because of opposing income and substitution effects. Under the assumptions leading to (37), these two effects exactly offset and the change in w_{t+1} has no impact on investment. This is the same reason that life-cycle saving behavior is independent of the interest rate when $\sigma = 1$.

28. (i) *Altruism: positive financial transfers* (see (33) and (34))

(a) An increase in the current generation's wealth will be partly shared with the future generations by increasing the financial transfer. Human capital investment would remain at the efficient level.

(b) To be careful, a clear answer to this question requires that we know what is causing the change in W_∞. For example, it could be due to higher future rental rates in human capital. Let's ignore this possibility for simplicity and think of it as a lump-sum change in the future generations' income. In this case, financial transfers would decrease, so that the parents can share in the family's greater resources, and human capital investments would stay at the efficient level.

(ii) *Altruism: zero financial transfers*

(a) An increase in the current generation's wealth will again be partly shared with the future generations by increasing human capital investment (see (37)).

(b) Under the assumption used to derive (37), we cannot think of the changes in W_∞ as resulting from lump sum changes in income. However, one can reason out the response to lump sum changes in future income using the general condition given by (26b). A rise in future income would increase the next generation's consumption on the left-hand side. This means that the right hand side must increase by reducing human capital investment and increasing the parent consumption.

(iii) *Warm glow* (see (39))

(a) An increase in the current generation's wealth will increase both types of intergenerational transfers

(b) An increase in the wealth of future generations does not impact the parents' behavior and both types of transfers remain the same.

29. Under warm glow, human capital investment is affected by parent's wealth because the adult human capital of children is a normal good that gives direct satisfaction to the parents. Under altruism, if the parents are constrained by their wealth level, human capital is also a function of parental wealth since this is the only way that an increase in wealth can be shared across generations. Thus, the warm glow assumption can be thought of as a simple way of modeling a wealth-constrained household with altruistic preferences.

30. Under altruism, human capital investment can never exceed the efficient level, provided the government does not subsidize the investment. Under warm-glow, if the utility benefit of increasing the child's adult human capital is sufficiently strong, then human capital investments can exceed the efficient level.

31. *G1* is explained by the fact that an increase in physical capital intensity only plays a small part of the economic growth in the United States. If k does not increase very much then the marginal product of capital and the return to capital will only be moderately higher in early periods of development compared to later periods.

G5 is explained by the fact that in United States history physical and human capital do a good job of explaining about half of the country's economic growth. The remaining half must be

Overlapping-Generations Model of Economic Growth

explained by technological progress or variables that we have to this point omitted from the model.

Problems

1. See section A.1 of the Technical Appendix for rules of differentiating power functions and section A.2 for a discussion of partial derivatives of functions with more than one independent variable.

Differentiation of (1), with respect to K and M, gives the marginal products of capital and labor $\partial Y_t / \partial K_t = \alpha A K_t^{\alpha-1} M_t^{1-\alpha}$ and $\partial Y_t / \partial M_t = (1-\alpha) A K_t^{\alpha} M_t^{-\alpha}$. Note that the exponent on K, in the marginal product of capital expression, and the exponent on M, in the marginal product of labor expression, are both negative. Thus, an increase in capital lowers the marginal product of capital and an increase in labor lowers the marginal product of labor.

See section A.1 of the Technical Appendix for a review of the algebra associated with power functions. If we scale the operation of the firm up or down by scaling the factors of production employed up or down by the factor κ, we have $A(\kappa K_t)^{\alpha}(\kappa M_t)^{1-\alpha} = A\kappa^{\alpha}(K_t)^{\alpha} \kappa^{1-\alpha}(M_t)^{1-\alpha} = \kappa A(K_t)^{\alpha}(M_t)^{1-\alpha} = \kappa Y_t$. Thus, we have scaled output up or down by the same factor—constant returns to scale.

2. The first order conditions for the firm are

(2.2a) $\alpha A K_t^{\alpha-1} M_t^{1-\alpha} = \alpha A k_t^{\alpha-1} = r_t$ and

(2.2b) $(1-\alpha) A K_t^{\alpha} M_t^{-\alpha} = (1-\alpha) A k_t^{\alpha} = w_t$.

Note that if we multiply both sides of (2.2a) by K and both sides of (2.2b) by M, we get (2.3a) and (2.3b). Thus, (2.3) follows directly from (2.2).

3. (a) $1 + r_t = (1.074)^{30} = 8.5139$, implying that $r_t = 7.5139$.

(b) From (2a) or (4), $k_t = \left(\dfrac{1/3}{7.5139}\right)^{1.5} = 0.0093$

(c) From (2b), $w_t = (1-\alpha) A k_t^{\alpha} = \dfrac{2}{3}(0.0093)^{1/3} = 0.1404$

(d) The assumption of perfect competition requires economic profit to always be zero.

Assuming that $A = 30$, changes (b) and (c). Now, we have

(b) $k_t = \left(\dfrac{10}{7.5139}\right)^{1.5} = 1.5353$

(c) $w_t = (1-\alpha) A k_t^{\alpha} = 20(1.5353)^{1/3} = 23.0723$

A higher value for A raises the marginal product of capital. The value of k_t must increase to drive the marginal product of capital back down to the given value of r_t. The increase in the marginal product of labor and w_t reflects the combined effects of a higher value of A and a higher value of k_t. Economic profit remains at zero because the value of w_t guarantees that the competition for the available labor eliminates all economic profit to capital owners.

4. The value of total income is $r_t K_t + w_t M_t$. The value of total output is $Y_t = \alpha Y_t + (1-\alpha)Y_t = r_t K_t + w_t M_t$, where the last equality follows from (2.3).

5. Household behavior is derived by solving the following constrained optimization problem (see the Technical Appendix A.2). Choose c_{1t} and c_{2t+1} to

Max $\ln c_{1t} + \beta \ln c_{2t+1}$ subject to $c_{1t} + \dfrac{c_{2t+1}}{R_t} = w_t$. The first order conditions are

$c_{1t}^{-1} = \lambda_t$ and $\beta c_{2t+1}^{-1} = \lambda_t / R_t$, where λ_t is the Lagrange multiplier associated with the constrained optimization problem. Use the first order conditions to solve for c_{2t+1} in terms of c_{1t} and substitute the solution into the lifetime budget constraint. Solve the lifetime budget constraint for c_{1t}. Substitute the solution into the first period budget constraint to solve for $s_t = w_t - c_{1t}$.

6. When R_t increases, the lifetime budget line pivots outward from its *fixed* intercept on the c_{1t}-axis (if the household has no saving, $c_{1t} = w_t$, then a higher interest on savings does not increase its consumption opportunities). Now, the household (a) can consume larger consumption bundles but (b) the opportunity cost of consuming a unit of c_{1t} is higher.

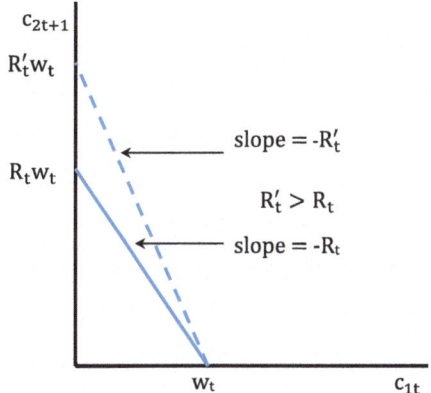

There is an *income or wealth effect* associated with (a) that indicates the household can afford more c_{1t}. However, the *substitution effect* associated with (b) creates an incentive to reduce c_{1t} in favor of c_{2t+1}. In (2.5a), these two conceptual effects exactly cancel and the optimal choice of c_{1t} is independent of the value of R_t.

7. The household behavior under this more general utility function is derived by solving the following constrained optimization problem (see the Technical Appendix A.2). Choose c_{1t} and c_{2t+1} to

Max $\dfrac{\left(c_{1t}^{1-1/\sigma} - 1\right) + \beta\left(c_{2t+1}^{1-1/\sigma}\right)}{1 - 1/\sigma}$, subject to $c_{1t} + \dfrac{c_{2t+1}}{R_t} = w_t$. The first order conditions are

$c_{1t}^{-1/\sigma} = \lambda_t$ and $\beta c_{2t+1}^{-1/\sigma} = \lambda_t / R_t$, where λ_t is the Lagrange multiplier associated with the constrained optimization problem. Use the first order conditions to solve for c_{2t+1} in terms of c_{1t} and substitute the solution into the lifetime budget constraint. Solve the lifetime budget constraint for c_{1t}. Substitute the solution into the first period budget constraint to solve for $s_t = w_t - c_{1t}$.

8. The supply of capital per worker in period t is $k_t^s \equiv s_{t-1} N_{t-1} / M_t^s = s_{t-1} N_{t-1} / N_t$

$= s_{t-1}/n$. Saving, from (2.6), is $s_{t-1} = \dfrac{\beta w_{t-1}}{1+\beta}$. Substituting for s_{t-1} in the definition for k_t^s yields (2.7).

9. The supply of capital per worker in period t is $k_t^s \equiv s_{t-1} N_{t-1} / M_t^s = s_{t-1} N_{t-1} / N_t$ $= s_{t-1}/n$. Saving, from *Problem 7*, is $s_{t-1} = \dfrac{\beta^\sigma R_{t-1}^{\sigma-1} w_{t-1}}{1 + \beta^\sigma R_{t-1}^{\sigma-1}} = \dfrac{w_{t-1}}{\beta^{-\sigma} R_{t-1}^{1-\sigma} + 1}$. Substituting for s_{t-1} in the definition for k_t^s, using definition of R_{t-1}, and the factor price equations from profit maximization yields the transition equation.

10. With technological progress, the definition of the supply of capital is $k_t^s \equiv s_{t-1} N_{t-1} / D_t N_t = (1/(1+\beta))(\beta w_{t-1} D_{t-1}) N_{t-1} / N_t D_t$. Simplifying and using the factor price equation for w_{t-1} gives (9).

11. The transition equation tells us k_t given the value of k_{t-1}. The fact that the exponent on k_{t-1} is less than one, implies the relationship between k_t and k_{t-1} is concave. The concave shape of the transition equation implies the transition equation must eventually cut the 45-degree line. This establishes the existence of a nontrivial steady state with $k > 0$. Technically the origin is also a steady state, but there is only one economically meaningful steady state.

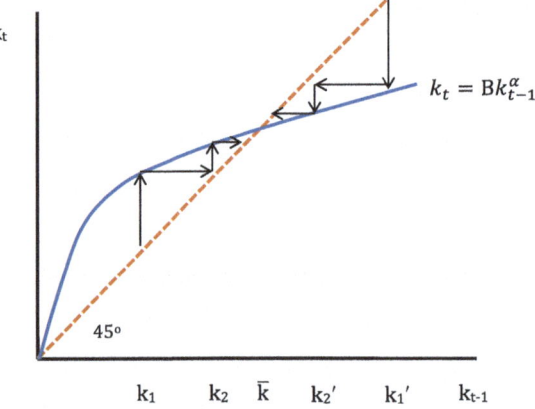

Furthermore, from tracing the dynamics using Figure 2, we know that no matter where the initial value of k is located, k_t will tend toward the unique non-zero steady state. This means the steady state is dynamically stable. Note that the origin is an unstable steady state because if

Overlapping-Generations Model of Economic Growth

the economy starts with a positive initial capital-labor ratio, no matter how small, it will move away from the origin toward the stable steady state with positive k. The global stability property is depicted here for initial values of k that are both smaller and greater than the steady state value.

12. Using (2.9), $k_t = \frac{\beta}{1+\beta} \frac{(1-\alpha)Ak_{t-1}^{\alpha}}{n(1+d)}$, we have

$k_1 = \frac{1}{3} \times \frac{2}{3} \times (0.05)^{1/3} = 0.0819$, $k_2 = 0.09651$, $k_3 = 0.1019$, $k_4 = 0.1038$, $k_5 = 0.1045$.

Solving (2.9) for $\bar{k}$ gives us $\bar{k} = \left[\frac{\beta}{1+\beta} \frac{(1-\alpha)A}{n(1+d)} \right]^{\frac{1}{1-\alpha}} = \left[\frac{1}{3} \times \frac{2}{3} \right]^{1.5} = 0.10476$.

13. $k_1 = 2.222 \times (0.05)^{1/3} = 0.8187$, $k_2 = 2.0789$, $k_3 = 2.8361$, $k_4 = 3.1454$, $k_5 = 3.2558$.

For the steady state, $\bar{k} = 3.3127$. A higher value of A increases the marginal product of labor, wages, and saving at any given level of capital intensity. This shifts the transition equation up, creating greater economic growth and a higher steady state capital-labor ratio. See the figure below for a diagrammatic depiction.

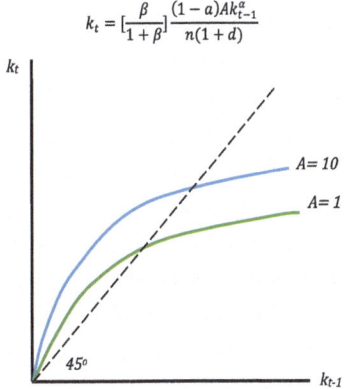

14. The transition path is $k_1 = \frac{1}{3} \times \frac{10}{1.5} \times \frac{2}{3} \times (0.05)^{1/3} = 0.5458$,

$k_2 = 1.4815 \times (0.5458)^{1/3} = 1.2108$, $k_3 = 1.5790$, $k_4 = 1.7251$, $k_5 = 1.7768$. For the steady state,

$\bar{k} = (1.4815)^{1.5} = 1.8032$. A higher value of n dilutes saving and the future capital created over more future workers. This shifts the transition equation down, creating a lower steady state capital-labor ratio.

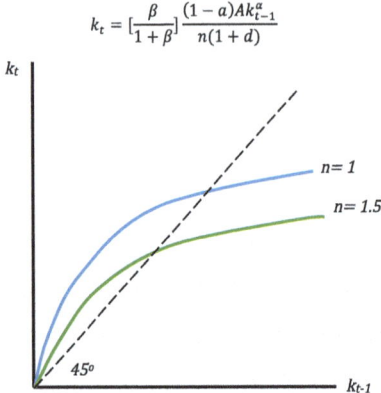

15. The increase in d creates the same path for k_t as in *Problem* 14. This is because $n = 1.5$ and $d = 0.5$ each imply the same growth in the *effective* labor force ($D_t M_t$) over time. Remember, $k_t = K_t / H_t \equiv K_t / D_t M_t$, so regardless of why H_t grows, it dilutes the value of k_t. The difference is that the growth in D_t, as opposed to growth in M_t, creates its own direct positive effect on worker productivity. An increase in d raises living standards, while an increase in n lowers them.

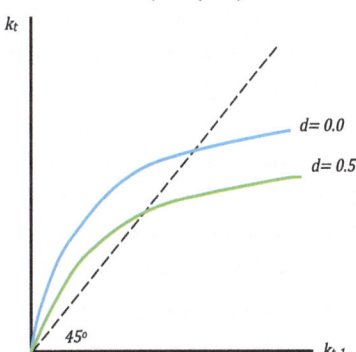

16. (a) $Y_t = AK_t^\alpha H_t^{1-\alpha} = AK_t^\alpha H_t^{-\alpha} H_t = A\left(\dfrac{K_t}{H_t}\right)^\alpha H_t = Ak_t^\alpha H_t$

(b) Because $H_t \equiv D_t M_t$, if we divide the expression for output in (a) by M_t, we get $\dfrac{Y_t}{M_t} = Ak_t^\alpha D_t$.

17. Substitute (2.10) into (2.2a) to get the steady state value for r_t, $\bar{r}$. Note that $\bar{r}$ does not depend on A. An increase in A directly *raises* the marginal product of capital for a given value of k but it also indirectly raises the steady state value of k, which *lowers* the marginal product of capital in the steady state. In the steady state, these two effects are exactly canceled.

To derive (13), solve the value for $\bar{r}$, from above, for the saving rate, $\dfrac{\beta}{1+\beta}$.

18. (a) If worker productivity increases 1.6 percent each year for 120 years then worker productivity in 1990 will be $(1.016)^{120} = 6.7181$ times higher than in 1870.

(b) To account for the rise in worker productivity, with equal contributions from physical capital accumulation and technical progress, technical progress must satisfy $D_{1990}/D_{1870} = (6.7181)^{1/2} = 2.5919$.

(c) The annual increase in labor productivity index needed to create a rise of 2.5919 over 120 years is $(2.5919)^{1/120} = 1.0079$. This means technical progress caused worker productivity to rise by 0.79 percent per year.

19. Here is a sketch of a program for computing the growth path. First, set the parameter values based on the calibration table and the initial guess for k in the first period. Then use (9) to write the transition equation as $k_t = 0.0445 k_{t-1}^{0.3333}$ and simulate a path of k values for at least four more periods. Next use (2.14) to check that the targeted total growth over the four periods has been met (a 2.59-fold increase in worker productivity). The initial guess for k suggested in the text is a good one, but the total growth was a little lower than the target (because k_5 does not actually reach $\bar{k}$, as was assumed to generate the guess). In this case you go back and make a new guess with a lower value for the initial k (less than 0.000538). An initial guess which gets us pretty close to the target is $k_1 = 0.00052$.

Use the associated path for k to compute $r_t - \delta$ for five periods (based on (2.2a)) and $\frac{(Y/M)_{t+1}}{(Y/M)_t}$ (based on (2.11)) for four periods (giving you the growth from one period to the next). Finally, compute the 5 *annualized* interest rates (rates of return to capital) and 4 *annualized* growth rates by using the equations: $(1+r_t-\delta)^{1/30} = 1 + annualized\ return$ and $\left[\frac{(Y/M)_{t+1}}{(Y/M)_t}\right]^{1/30} = 1 + annualized\ growth\ rate$. For the initial guess mentioned above, the interest rates are 14.03, 9.28, 7.75, 7.25, and 7.08 percent and the growth rates are 2.97, 1.52, 1.04, and 0.87 percent.

20. The procedure sketched in the answer to problem 19 is used to answer Problem 20. The difference is that, after the initial period, the value for k must be computed using a nonlinear equation solver that numerically computes a value for k that approximately satisfies the transition equation when $\sigma \neq 1$. For $\sigma = 0.5$, the transition takes slightly longer to reach the steady state and a lower value of the initial k must be chosen. An initial $k = 0.00048$ works pretty well. In this case, the simulated interest rates are 14.3, 10.3, 8.5, 7.7, 7.3 and the growth rates are 2.57, 1.64, 1.20, 0.98. The growth rates sequence is improved somewhat because the growth rates do not fall as sharply as when $\sigma = 1$, but is not much better. When $\sigma < 1$, saving rates increase as the returns to capital fall, helping to strengthen capital accumulation and growth.

21. With $\delta = 1$ and $\sigma = \frac{2-\alpha}{1-\alpha}$, we can write the transition equation from *Problem 9* as $k_t = \frac{(1-\alpha)Ak_{t-1}^\alpha}{n(1+d)} \frac{1}{1+\beta^{-\sigma}(\alpha A)^{1-\sigma} k_t}$. This expression can be written as $\beta^{-\sigma}(\alpha A)^{1-\sigma} k_t^2 + k_t + \frac{-(1-\alpha)Ak_{t-1}^\alpha}{n(1+d)} = 0$, which is a quadratic equation in the unknown k_t. Applying the quadratic formula, see the Technical Appendix, reveals that there is only one

positive solution, $k_t = \dfrac{\left(1 + 4\dfrac{\beta^{-\sigma}(\alpha A)^{1-\sigma}(1-\alpha)Ak_{t-1}^{\alpha}}{n(1+d)}\right)^{1/2} - 1}{2\beta^{-\sigma}(\alpha A)^{1-\sigma}}$. Note that when $k_{t-1} = 0$, then $k_t = 0$. Also differentiating twice with respect to k_{t-1} reveals that $dk_t/dk_{t-1} > 0$ and $d^2k_t/dk_{t-1}^2 < 0$. Thus, the transition function is a concave function emanating from the origin.

22. First, use (2.22b) to eliminate c_{2t+1} in (2.27a). Next, substitute (2.32) into (2.27a) to eliminate c_{1t}, and then solve for nb_{t+1} to get (2.33). The financial transfer under warm glow follows directly from the solution to the optimization problem.

23. Complete hints for the derivation are provided in the question.

24. (i) $V_{t+1}(W_{t+1}) = E + \left[\dfrac{1+\beta}{1-\beta\theta}\right]\ln W_{t+1} + \beta\left(\Phi_{t+1}^R + \left[\dfrac{1+\beta}{1-\beta\theta}\right]\Phi_{t+1}^w\right)$

(ii) $V_t(W_t) = U_t + \beta\left(E + \left[\dfrac{1+\beta}{1-\beta\theta}\right]\ln W_{t+1} + \beta\left(\Phi_{t+1}^R + \left[\dfrac{1+\beta}{1-\beta\theta}\right]\Phi_{t+1}^w\right)\right)$

(iii) $U_t = \ln c_{1t} + \beta \ln c_{2t+1}$

$\quad = \ln c_{1t} + \beta \ln \dfrac{\psi_{2t}}{\psi_{1t}} c_{1t}$

$\quad = (1+\beta)\ln c_{1t} + \beta \ln R_t + \beta \ln \beta$

From the budget constraints we also have $c_{1t} = \dfrac{W_t - nx_t}{1+\beta}$, so

$U_t = (1+\beta)\ln\left(\dfrac{W_t - nx_t}{1+\beta}\right) + \beta \ln R_t + \beta \ln \beta$

(iv) Note that $W_{t+1} = w_{t+1}\Theta x_t^\theta$. The objective function can now be written solely in terms of exogenous variables and the choice variable x_t,

$V_t(W_t) = (1+\beta)\ln\left(\dfrac{W_t - nx_t}{1+\beta}\right) + \beta \ln R_t + \beta \ln \beta +$

$\beta\left(E + \left[\dfrac{1+\beta}{1-\beta\theta}\right]\ln\left(w_{t+1}\Theta x_t^\theta\right) + \beta\left(\Phi_{t+1}^R + \left[\dfrac{1+\beta}{1-\beta\theta}\right]\Phi_{t+1}^w\right)\right).$

Write out the portion of the objective function involving x_{t+1} and maximize with respect to x_{t+1} to get (2.37)

(v) Now substitute the solution back into the objective function to get

$$V_t(W_t) = (1+\beta)\ln\left(\frac{(1-\beta\theta)W_t}{1+\beta}\right) + \beta \ln R_t + \beta \ln \beta +$$

$$\beta\left(E + \left[\frac{1+\beta}{1-\beta\theta}\right]\ln\left(w_{t+1}\Theta\left(\frac{\beta\theta W_t}{n}\right)^\theta\right) + \beta\left(\Phi_{t+1}^R + \left[\frac{1+\beta}{1-\beta\theta}\right]\Phi_{t+1}^w\right)\right).$$

Write out the right hand side of the objective function as instructed in the question,

$$(1+\beta)\ln\left(\frac{1-\beta\theta}{1+\beta\theta}\right) + \beta \ln \beta + \beta E + \beta\frac{1+\beta}{1-\beta\theta}\left(\ln \Theta + \theta \ln \frac{\beta\theta}{n}\right)$$

$$+ \frac{1+\beta}{1-\beta\theta}\ln W_t$$

$$+ \beta\left(\ln R_t + \beta\Phi_{t+1}^R\right)$$

$$+ \beta\frac{1+\beta}{1-\beta\theta}\left(\ln w_{t+1} + \beta\Phi_{t+1}^w\right).$$

Note that the first expression, involving all constant terms, must equal E and can be solved for the value of E that satisfies the equality. The second term is just as stated in (2.36). Recognizing that $\left(\ln R_t + \beta\Phi_{t+1}^R\right) = \Phi_t^R$ and $\left(\ln w_{t+1} + \beta\Phi_{t+1}^w\right) = \Phi_t^w$, completes the proof.

25. First, simplify the aggregate consumption expression as,
$$\frac{C_t}{M_t} = \frac{N_t c_{1t} + N_{t-1} c_{2t}}{N_t} = c_{1t} + \frac{c_{2t}}{n} = \psi_{1t} w_t + R_{t-1}(s_{t-1}/n) = \psi_{1t} w_t + R_{t-1} k_t.$$

Next, substitute the new expression for aggregate consumption into the transition equation to get
$$nk_{t+1} = Ak_t^\alpha + (1-\delta)k_t - \psi_{1t}(1-\alpha)Ak_t^\alpha - (1+\alpha k_t^{\alpha-1} - \delta)k_t$$

$$= \frac{(1-\alpha)Ak_t^\alpha}{1+\beta^{-\sigma}\left(1+\alpha k_{t+1}^\alpha - \delta\right)^{1-\sigma}}.$$

Chapter 3
Fiscal Policy

Reader's Guide

Section 3.1   Introducing the Government

Purpose: From Chapter 2 we learned that investments in physical and human capital explained about half of US historical growth. In Chapter 3 we consider a third investment leading to US growth—government investment in infrastructure and basic research (a key determinant of technical progress). However, we also acknowledge when government policies may reduce economic growth.

Sticking Points: (i) Perhaps the most important new modeling twist is to introduce the positive effect of public capital on worker productivity by making D_t now partly endogenous and partly exogenous. This is done by writing, $D_t = E_t g_t^{\mu}$, where g_t is a measure of how much public capital there is per worker and μ is a parameter gauging the impact of public capital on worker productivity. The new variable E_t takes on the interpretation we previously gave to D_t, an index capturing how unexplained advances in technology affect worker productivity (note that D_t collapses to E_t if $\mu = 0$).

(ii) How does the government potentially *lower* productivity? There are three ways this can happen.
- taxing wages, which lowers the household income that funds saving and private capital formation
- using tax revenue for the purchase of government consumption goods rather than investment goods
- using tax revenue to hire government officials, thereby diverting labor away from the production of private goods.

To promote growth and development, the government must do a good job balancing these different actions with government investment.

Take Away: This section allows us to consider how several important features of government behavior affect the economy's growth: investment in public capital, purchasing consumption goods and services, and taxation.

Sections 3.2.1-3.2.3   *Government Consumption*

Purpose: Examine how private capital formation is affected when the government raises taxes to buy consumer goods or hire government workers/officials.

Sticking Points   (i) It's important to remember that we focus solely on *private* production. There are important services that enhance people's welfare from government activity that are hard to measure but nevertheless real. For example, the military is needed for national defense and the provision of that security generates welfare. However, we are only looking at the *costs* of hiring, clothing, feeding, and equipping the soldiers on the production of private goods and services and not on the private consumption *benefits* that come from greater security.

(ii) The effect of taxing to hire government workers, surprisingly, has no effect on the private capital supplied to private sector workers. Taxing private sector workers to pay for government workers certainly lowers the saving of these households. However, the tax revenue is paid out to government workers and they save for retirement as well. Thus, the total saving and the capital it finances are unaffected.

Take-Away: The combined effect of government taxation used to purchase consumption goods and hire workers lowers output by lowering private capital accumulation and by diverting labor away from private production.

Section 3.2.4   *Government Investment*

Purpose: Add an additional type of investment that extends our ability to explain growth and development.

Sticking Points: (i) Public capital directly raises productivity via the term $D_t = E_t g_t^\mu$ but can also indirectly raise or lower productivity through effects on private capital accumulation. Effects on k_t :

- positive effect #1—public capital complements private capital in production, an effect that shows up by raising the exponent on k_t in the transition equation for k_{t+1} (from α to $\alpha + \mu(1-\alpha)$), thereby weakening diminishing returns
- positive effect #2—public capital raises worker productivity and wages which increases pre-tax saving
- negative effect #1—public capital investments are funded by raising taxes which lowers after-tax saving.

The interaction of the last two effects is tricky and deserves its own Sticking Points entry.

(ii) When taxes are used to fund government investment there is a "humped-shaped" non-monotonic relationship between taxes and private capital accumulation

Fiscal Policy

(and, in turn, worker productivity). When taxes are low, and public capital is scarce, the marginal product of public capital is high. Raising taxes in the low-tax range generates enough of a payoff from government investment that the gain in worker productivity is larger than the negative effect of taxes, causing after-tax wages, saving, and private capital accumulation to rise. As taxes and public capital increase, the marginal product of further investment weakens and the effect of more public capital is too weak to offset the negative effect of taxes, causing after-tax wages, saving, and private capital accumulation to fall. These effects are contained in the κ coefficient in equation (3.14).

Take-Away   The most important implication of our analysis of government investment is that it helps explain why during early and middle stages of growth, the economy's growth rate can be maintained at a trendless rate. As long as the return to investment in public capital such as roads, utilities, education, and basic research remains high, an economy can keep growing because expanding government investment not only directly raises worker productivity but also keeps private capital accumulation going. In this way, public capital offsets the diminishing returns that would occur from private capital accumulation alone. This is the analytical argument behind the conjecture from the end of section 2.4 of Chapter 2 that to explain historical growth in the US, one needs to include the effects of public capital.

Section 3.4   *Pure and Impure Public Capital*

Purpose: Many types of public capital are also "public goods." How does this affect the interpretation of our model?

Sticking Points: (i) A pure public good generates the same individual benefits independent of how many people are consuming/using it (think national defense). We treat public capital as a private good. Typically, the most appropriate assumption is that public capital is something in between, an impure public good where crowding can occur that reduces individual benefits as total consumption/use rises but everyone gets some benefit simultaneously.

(ii) How to model an impure public good? Let the individual productivity benefits of public capital be determined by G_t / N_t^{ξ}, where $1 \geq \xi \geq 0$. If $\xi = 1$ then G_t is a pure private good. If $\xi = 0$ then G_t is a pure public good. The case with greatest applicability is when $1 > \xi > 0$, an impure public good.

(iii) With an impure public good, the expression for the productivity index is $D_t = \bar{E}_t g_t^{\mu}$, where g_t is defined as before but now $\bar{E}_t \equiv E_t N_t^{(1-\xi)\mu}$. A larger population means productivity rises, for a given value of g_t, because of the sharing effect enjoyed by all households. The sharing effect is larger the closer ξ is to zero. Worker productivity is higher in larger communities despite similar public capital per household.

Take-Away: Treating public capital as an impure public good is possible without changing the basic characteristics of our model with the exception that the productivity index will vary positively with population size.

Section 3.5   Open Economy

Purpose: The analysis of Chapter 2, and Chapter 3 up to this point, assumes the economy being studied is perfectly closed from international trading of goods and assets. We now think about how growth is affected by opening a country's borders to capital flows.

Sticking Points   (i) Most countries have to initiate their growth and development in a closed economy context. This is difficult because domestic saving is too low to finance all of the high return investment projects they need. Opening the economy to capital flows has the potential advantage of attracting saving from other countries to finance those investments.

(ii) In an open economy, capital accumulation differs dramatically from a closed economy because national saving no longer becomes the key determinant of growth. This means that the transition equation that is built on the capital market equilibrium between domestic investment and national saving no longer applies. In an open economy, as long as the return to capital investment (the MPK) is high, capital will quickly accumulate independent of national saving, as foreign saving will pour into a country to take advantage of investment opportunities. However, this requires the developing country to establish the prerequisites for a high MPK.

(iii) The prerequisites for a high MPK are the factors other than private capital that affect capital productivity. These other factors are A and g; a country must create an attractive environment for private business by having reasonable laws, sound infrastructure, and and at least a literate and numerate work force. The influence of A and g on attracting private capital can be seen in equation (3.18), which takes over for the transition equation as the equation that determines a country's private capital intensity in an open economy.

(iv) An important topic, neglected in the reading, is the taxation of capital income in an open economy. Taxing capital income has the danger of causing capital flight. This was one of the main motivations for the 2017-2018 tax cuts on corporate profit in the US. It is easy to adjust our model for the taxation of capital income as indicated in *Problem 18*.

Take-Away   If an economy can open its borders to capital flows, then the growth-promoting strategy shifts from trying to encourage domestic saving to making the country an attractive place for investments from all over the world. This creates the potential for more rapid development than is possible in a closed economy. More discussion of development in an open economy is found in Chapters 5 and 11.

Fiscal Policy

Section 3.6 Endogenous Fiscal Policy

Purpose: This section shows how fiscal policy can be made endogenous (explained with the theory) by modeling public officials and their policy choices.

Sticking Points: (i) To capture why governments choose different fiscal policies, we need to distinguish consumption benefits to public officials (salaries and perks of office) from policy benefits enjoyed by private households. We assume public officials have preferences that include both, $\ln c_t^g + \phi U_t$, where c_t^g is consumption benefits of the official and U_t is our usual lifetime utility of the generation-t household. The preference parameter ϕ determines how altruistic or benevolent the officials are, which drives their policy choices.

(ii) A complication is that there is no natural time horizon for the officials because policies should be forward looking to some extent. For example, pro-growth governments care about the welfare of future generations and not only the welfare of generations currently alive. This consideration leads to the objective function given by (3.25).

(iii) Despite the complex objective function, the optimal fiscal policy from the policy makers' perspective turns out to be simple and intuitive, as seen by (3.27a) and (3.27b).

Take-Away: Fiscal policies vary across countries, as more benevolent governments choose lower tax rates and use more of their tax revenue for government investment. Fiscal policy differences lead to significant but not large differences in worker productivity and welfare. This topic is explored further in Chapter 5.

Section 3.7-3.8 Convergence

Purpose: Diminishing returns to investments can only be postponed by raising investment rates for so long. Once the investment rates stop rising, growth will slow. These sections draw out further implications of diminishing returns. See Chapter 12 for more details.

Sticking Points (i) Rich countries have to face the fact that further growth is going to be difficult. Since the 1970s, developed economies have seen a steady decline in the growth rate of worker productivity. In the US, the growth rate has fallen more than a percentage point from almost 3 percent to about half that value. Growth slowdowns are inevitable because of diminishing returns. As the physical and human capital stock of countries rise, the return on investments that attempt to increase them further become smaller. The same rate of investment leads to weaker gains in output and income.

In addition, as countries become richer, they tend to increase the fraction of output devoted to consumption and lower their saving and investment rates. Social insurance programs for retirees lower saving and the funding needed for private capital investment. These programs also chew up bigger fractions of government budgets that could have been spent on government investment in public capital such as infrastructure and basic research. Education policy has become overly concentrated on consumption benefits associated with the minority of the population that attends and graduates from four-year colleges. College standards are falling, reducing the skills learned by the highly educated. The focus on college also causes too little investment in developing skills of most of the workforce.

(ii) One implication of diminishing returns is that poor countries have the potential to grow faster than rich countries. If this is true then, over the course of time, worker productivity and living standards should *converge* across the world as poorer countries *catch-up* to richer countries.

(iii) While rapid convergence has occurred for a small set of less developed countries over the second half of the 20th century, on average we have *not* seen poor countries converge to the living standards of richer countries.

(iv) Comparisons of living standards over time and across countries are typically based on worker productivity or GDP per capita. However, economic welfare depends on many factors that cannot be fully traded in markets: health and longevity, home production, and the quality of the environment. Personal safety and security and equality of opportunity also affect individual welfare but are missing from GDP calculations as they depend on depend on public governance and the quality of social norms and formal and informal institutions rather than market transactions.

Recent research constructs a comprehensive measure of individual welfare by country. The research finds that welfare determinants, while not explicitly included in GDP measures, may be correlated with income in the sense that richer countries have more amenities and nonmarket benefits. In fact, the welfare gaps across countries are much larger than the income gaps. For example, while a U.S. household has almost 17 times higher income than a household living in Sub-Saharan Africa, the welfare gap in consumption-equivalent units is 33 when using the broadest collection of welfare determinants. Furthermore, while income gaps between advanced countries and Africa exhibit painfully slow convergence, welfare gaps have *diverged* over the last 30 years.

More complete studies also impute welfare losses from global CO_2 emissions. Based on evidence from historical temperature shocks, the cost of emissions are computed throughout the life of a representative household in each country. Emissions lead to higher temperatures and lower output and consumption. The measured effects are country-specific because the negative effects from rising temperatures and changing precipitation have an empirical relationship with a country's GDP. Across the globe, climate change lowers welfare relative to the United States, a factor causing welfare to diverge further as we move forward in time.

Take-Away: There is the *potential* for living standards across the world to converge. It has not generally happened because many developing countries get trapped in low-productivity steady states. We will see the details of how this happens in Chapters 4-6.

Solutions to Exercises

Questions

1. The budget constraint is $\tau_t w_t D_t (1+\varsigma) N_t = C_t^g + w_t D_t \varsigma N_t + G_{t+1}$. On the left-hand-side, we have sources of funds and on the right-hand-side, uses.

Sources of Funds
$\tau_t w_t D_t (1+\varsigma) N_t$—wage taxes

Uses of Funds
C_t^g—expenditures on private consumption goods (government consumption purchases)

$w_t D_t \varsigma N_t$—wages paid to government officials (government consumption purchases)

G_{t+1}—public capital expenditures (government investment purchases)

2. Government capital is a complementary input to private capital and labor that impacts production via the labor productivity index. The funds for government investment are generated as the difference between wage taxes and government consumption purchases. The dependence of government investment on wages causes government capital to move proportionally with the private physical capital stock because private saving is also proportional to wages.

3. A new source of worker productivity is public capital per worker. Public capital complements the determinants of worker productivity from Chapter 2: TFP, technology, and private capital. We now also include the presence of government officials. Government employees do not contribute to measured production in our model. The larger is employment in the public sector, the lower is private output per worker across the entire economy.

4. (a) When taxes are raised to finance consumption, the after-tax wage and saving of the private households fall. Less saving means less private capital formation and lower worker productivity.
    (b) When taxes are raised to finance employment there is no effect on aggregate saving in the economy because government workers save at the same rate as private sector workers (any redistribution of income across workers in the public and private sectors does not change total saving). However, private production is now spread across private and public workers causing output per worker to fall.
    (c) When taxes are raised to finance government investment there are two opposing effects on production in the long run. More public capital raises production but less saving lowers private capital and production. At relatively low tax rates the net effect is positive (because the

return to public capital is relatively high) but if taxes become too high the net effect can be negative. See *Problems* 4, 8-10 for more on this trade-off.

5.   With public capital, the transition equation for private capital takes the form $k_{t+1} = \kappa k_t^{\alpha + \mu(1-\alpha)}$, where κ is made up of various constant parameters from the model as well as the tax rate τ. One important thing to notice about the transition equation is that the exponent on k_t has increased. The larger exponent makes the transition equation less concave and reduces the growth slowdown as capital accumulates. The sharply diminishing output growth rates and interest rates were problematic predictions of the neoclassical growth model. The fact that public capital rises with private capital reduces this problem by raising the marginal product of private capital and labor. This helps smooth growth rates over the transition to the steady state, thereby providing a better fit to the historical experience of developing economies.

A second feature of the transition equation involves the coefficient κ. As highlighted in *Problems* 8-11, κ is a concave function of the tax rate used to finance government investment in public capital. At low tax rates and low levels of investment, additional investment has a big payoff to productivity causing κ to rise with τ. This means the transition equation has the potential to shift up in early stages of development, maintaining the growth rate in the capital-labor ratio and worker productivity.

6.   The empirical studies primarily use a narrow definition of public capital based on physical infrastructure such as roads. The studies use regression analysis to statistically estimate the parameter μ —the output elasticity associated with public capital. Most studies estimate μ to fall in a range from 0.20 to 0.40.

7.   A *pure public good* provides the same benefits to the individual, independent of how many other individuals are also being served, i.e. there is no crowding effect that reduces benefits as the number of consumers increases. The classic example of a public good is the provision of national defense. An *impure public good* can serve many households at the same time but with some reduction of individual benefits as the number of total consumers increases. Public roads are a good example. With a *purely private good*, if one individual uses the good, no other individual receives any direct benefits.

The production function in (3.2) assumes that the government capital is a private good—to maintain its productivity effect, the amount of capital services must rise proportionally with the number of workers. Security protection of a business from theft, fire, or disputed liabilities involving the court system come closest to being private services provided by the government. Most government capital provides service flows that are impure public goods, such as public education, public roads, and public utilities.

Equation (3.16) is used to generalize the production function when government capital is an impure public good that includes the private and pure public good possibilities as special cases. Equation (3.16) shows that the general case can be put in the same form as (3.3) but where TFP must be re-interpreted to include a population size dimension. If government capital is an impure public good then, for a given ratio of public capital to workers, countries with larger populations have higher TFP as workers can share the productivity effects of the government capital made available.

8. In the closed economy, physical capital must be funded by national saving. In a small open economy, national saving plays no role in domestic physical capital formation. Funding for domestic investment will be provided by foreign countries if the return to investment is attractive. The key to generating high physical capital intensity in an open economy is to have a high marginal product of capital due to high levels of TFP or government infrastructure.

9. The domestic marginal product of the capital ($\alpha A g_t^{\mu(1-\alpha)} k_t^{\alpha-1}$) is decreasing in k_t, so its plot is downward sloping. The value of r^* is independent of k_t, so its plot is a horizontal line that maintains a fixed value. The intersection of these two plots identifies the open economy equilibrium value of k_t given in (3.18).

Whether k_t becomes higher or lower in an open economy depends on whether the marginal product of capital in the closed economy is higher or lower than r^*. If A and g_t are low in a country then the closed economy marginal product may be lower than r^*. In this case, k_t will *fall back* from its closed economy value and move toward the open-economy intersection point, as indicated in the figure below. Capital flight occurs as private capital owners seek higher returns (r^*) in other countries.

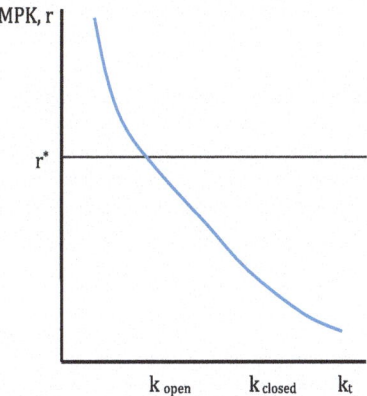

10. (a) The parameter ϕ captures the concern the government has for the welfare of private citizens. As the kelptocracy becomes more selfish, the value of ϕ falls.

(b) The tax rate, τ, and ϕ are inversely related. Thus, a lower value of ϕ causes τ to increase.

(c) An increase in τ lowers private saving and the steady state capital intensity, $\bar{k}$, falls.

(d) An increase in τ raises tax revenue but the government also lowers the fraction of tax revenue invested in public capital to maintain a constant rate of investment out of national income. The decrease in the private capital intensity lowers national income, causing public capital intensity, $\bar{g}$, to fall as well.

(e) The decline in both $\bar{k}$ and $\bar{g}$ implies that $\bar{y}$ falls as τ increases.

11. In a *dictatorship*, the country's leader has complete power to set policy. A dictator may be quite altruistic, with a high value of ϕ placed on the welfare of private citizens, possibly higher than in a democracy. A kleptocracy is a special case of dictatorship where the value of ϕ is low.

12. The value of τ^R is chosen to match the relatively low fraction of output that is devoted to government purchases in some rich countries, such as the U.S., where the government purchase share of output is between 15 and 20 percent. The value of τ^P is chosen to match the relatively high government purchase share in some poor countries, which Table 1 indicates can be between 30 and 35 percent. Even if we chose a large gap in government purchases shares, with $\tau^R = 0.15$ and $\tau^P = 0.35$, the worker productivity of the rich countries is 30 percent higher than that of the poor country, far short of the massive gaps observed in the data. High taxes and government purchases shares significantly lower output but cannot alone explain income gaps across countries.

13. Higher values of α and μ cause more long-run capital accumulation and a higher state level of worker productivity because diminishing returns is not as severe (steeper transition equation plots with less curvature). This result also implies that high tax rates, via their negative effect on capital accumulation, have a larger long-run negative effect on worker productivity.

Estimates of α and μ are based on the standard definition of tangible physical capital. Broader notions of capital include *intangible* capital that can increase estimates of α and μ. Intangible capital is knowledge about production and effective governance that results from investment of resources.

14. Standard measures of government physical capital tend to underestimate the true differences across rich and poor countries. Measures of government capital are based on the budgets for government investment projects such as roads. However, some of the budgeted funds are never invested because they are instead diverted to public officials and private

Fiscal Policy 39

contractors for consumption. The variable u represents the fraction of the budget that is diverted away from its intended purpose.

Poor countries generally are less effective at checking corruption than rich countries, so their values of u are higher. This means that the actual gaps in public capital intensities across rich and poor countries are larger than the measured gaps.

15. Growth theory says there are diminishing returns to accumulating more capital per worker because the worker's capacity to use the capital is limited. The limits of human ability to learn also suggest that there are diminishing returns to human capital investments. This principle applies to a given individual that tries to learn more advanced knowledge and to a society that tries to instill a given level of knowledge and skills in larger fractions of its population.

16. As discussed in *Question* 15, diminishing returns from capital accumulation cause growth to slow down *for a given rate of investment*. Developed economies have also experienced a decline in their saving and investment rates, further contributing to the slowdown. One reason for the decline in the saving rate across developed countries is the expansion of PAYG programs for retirees. PAYG financing schemes tax workers, who are consuming at a relatively low rate, and transfers the funds to retirees who are consuming at a relatively high rate. The intergenerational redistribution of income causes the national consumption rate to rise and the national saving rate to fall. See Chapter 12 for more details.

17. "Crowding out" refers to the reduction in investment associated with increased government borrowing. As governments attempt to borrow more from financial markets, they are forced to raise interest rates to attract additional household saving. To compete, firms must do the same, which makes the costs of borrowing to finance investment projects higher. The higher interest cost causes some investment projects to be cancelled or scaled back.

Given the large amounts the governments in richer countries are borrowing, it is surprising that interest rates have remained low. This is due to the willingness of high-saving countries, e.g. Japan and China, to lend their savings internationally. As a result, the government borrowing binge has, thus far, not resulted in significantly higher interest rates and lower private investment. Recently rates are on the rise, so the period of cheap credit may be over.

Government borrowing also has the potential to crowd out future government investment. Increased borrowing today, to finance transfer programs or low taxes, raises the government's debt obligations in the future. More of the future government budgets must be devoted to pay the principal and interest on previously issued debt, leaving fewer discretionary funds for government investment projects.

18. The average years of schooling for workers in rich countries continues to increase but the rate of increase has slowed. Among OECD countries, average years of schooling increased from 10 to 12 over the last 25 years. Predictions are that it will take twice as long for average years to increase from 12 to 14. In the first half of the post WWII period, average years of schooling across birth cohorts in the United States rose by 2.3 years. Since then, years of schooling have

risen by less than 1 year. The four-year college enrollment and completion rates for students of traditional college age have completely stalled. The modest rise in years of schooling is due to increased enrollment in two-year schools and increased college attendance and completion of older students.

The quality of education has also slipped because of falling standards in college courses. This is consistent with the fact that real wages of workers with only an undergraduate degree have been falling in recent years.

19. Optimism stems from further advances in computing and artificial intelligence that could raise productivity through enhanced robotics, 3D printing that adds the design and production of new products, and the ability to organize and analyze large data sets. Pessimists argue that artificial intelligence has been advancing for some time, while the rate of technological progress has remained weak. The pessimists also point out that the rate of innovation more generally peaked early in the 20th century and that government support for basic research has fallen since the second half of the 20th century.

20. *G1* says that, despite industrialization and the physical capital accumulation associated with development, the return to capital only falls moderately. The marginal product of capital fails to fall dramatically because human capital and public capital also rise in a growing economy. Higher values of these complementary inputs raise the productivity of physical capital and limit the force of diminishing marginal productivity.

Public infrastructure provided by the government is necessary for modern growth to occur. Without roads, public schooling, and well-established property rights the returns to private investment is too low and too risky. All Growth Miracles received a strong push from government investment. In some cases, the government not only fails to provide the needed infrastructure but also fails to provide internal security. Civil unrest and even wars disrupt an economy, leading to Growth Disasters. Variation in government performance is an important reason for the variation in growth rates noted in *G6*.

Problems

1. Follow the same approach used to answer *Problem 5* of Chapter 2. Set up and maximize the following Lagrangian, $\ln c_{1t} + \beta \ln c_{2t+1} + \lambda_t \left[(1-\tau_t)w_t D_t - c_{1t} - \frac{c_{2t+1}}{R_t} \right]$.

2. Under the assumptions of the problem, the capital market equilibrium condition (3.7) becomes $K_{t+1} = Ns_t = N \frac{\beta}{1+\beta}(1-\tau_t)w_t$. Dividing by the private sector workforce, $(1-\varepsilon)N$, to form the capital-labor ratio gives us $k_{t+1} = \frac{1}{1-\varepsilon}\frac{\beta}{1+\beta}(1-\tau_t)w_t = \frac{1}{1-\varepsilon}\frac{\beta}{1+\beta}(w_t - \tau_t w_t)$.

Substituting the government budget constraint, where the only expense is paying public

Fiscal Policy

employees, $\tau_t w_t N = w_t \varepsilon N$ or $\tau_t w_t = w_t \varepsilon$, into the capital market equilibrium condition above yields

$$k_{t+1} = \frac{1}{1-\varepsilon}\frac{\beta}{1+\beta}(w_t - \tau_t w_t) = \frac{1}{1-\varepsilon}\frac{\beta}{1+\beta}w_t(1-\varepsilon) = \frac{\beta}{1+\beta}Ak_t^\alpha,\text{ the same as (3.10)}.$$

Furthermore, private output per worker in the economy as a whole is

$$y_t = \frac{Y_t}{N} = \frac{AK_t^\alpha\left((1-\varepsilon)N\right)^{1-\alpha}}{N} = Ak_t^\alpha(1-\varepsilon).$$ Although a slightly different form than under the approach used in the text to introduce government employment, the message is the same: an increase in ε lowers worker productivity.

3. To derive each transition equation begin by substituting (3.3), (3.4b), and (3.6c) into (3.7) to get

$$K_{t+1} = (1+\varsigma)N_t\frac{\beta(1-\tau_t)w_t D_t}{1+\beta}.$$

Under the assumptions made in sections 3.1-3.2, the equation can be written as

$$K_{t+1} = (1+\varsigma)N_t\frac{\beta}{1+\beta}(1-\tau_t)(1-\alpha)Ag_t^{\mu(1-\alpha)}k_t^\alpha$$

or

$$(*)\quad k_{t+1} = (1+\varsigma)\frac{\beta}{1+\beta}(1-\tau_t)(1-\alpha)Ag_t^{\mu(1-\alpha)}k_t^\alpha.$$

This is the general transition equation for all applications in the chapter. Now on to the special cases.

To derive (3.9), assume $\mu = \varsigma = 0$ and $\tau_t w_t = c_t^g$ to convert (*) to

$$k_{t+1} = \frac{\beta}{1+\beta}\left[(1-\alpha)Ak_t^\alpha - \tau_t(1-\alpha)Ak_t^\alpha\right]$$

or

$$(9)\quad k_{t+1} = \frac{\beta}{1+\beta}\left[(1-\alpha)Ak_t^\alpha - c_t^g\right].$$

To derive (3.10), use $\mu = 0$ and $\tau_t = \varsigma/(1+\varsigma)$ to convert (*) to

$$k_{t+1} = (1+\varsigma)\frac{\beta}{1+\beta}(1-\frac{\varsigma}{1+\varsigma})(1-\alpha)Ak_t^\alpha$$

or

$$(10)\quad k_{t+1} = \frac{\beta}{1+\beta}(1-\alpha)Ak_t^\alpha.$$

To derive (3.14), assume $\tau_t = \tau$, $\varsigma = 0$, and $\tau w_t D_t N = G_{t+1}$. Using (13), (*) can be written as

$$k_{t+1} = \frac{\beta}{1+\beta}(1-\tau)(1-\alpha)A\left[\frac{\tau}{1-\tau}\frac{1+\beta}{\beta}k_t\right]^{\mu(1-\alpha)} k_t^\alpha = (1-\alpha)A\left[\frac{\beta(1-\tau)}{1+\beta}\right]^{1-\mu(1-\alpha)} \tau^{\mu(1-\alpha)} k_t^{\alpha+\mu(1-\alpha)}$$

or

(14) $\quad k_{t+1} = \kappa k_t^{\alpha+\mu(1-\alpha)}$.

4. After taking the natural log of the RHS of (3.14), the only terms involving τ_t are $(1-\mu(1-\alpha))\ln(1-\tau_t) + \mu(1-\alpha)\ln(\tau_t)$. Taking the derivative with respect to τ_t, setting the derivative expression equal to zero, and solving for the tax rate yields, $\tau_t = \tau = \mu(1-\alpha)$.

5. For α = 2/3, $\beta = 0.8400$, and with the other parameter settings from section 2.4 of Chapter 2, the numerical transition equation is $k_t = 0.0889 k_{t-1}^{0.6667}$. Starting with the given initial value of $k_1 = 0.0001155$, subsequent values for k can now be generated. As in *Problem 19* from Chapter 2 you can use these values to compute
(i) annualized worker productivity growth rates across periods:

$$\left(\left[\left(\frac{k_{t+1}}{k_t}\right)^\alpha (1+d)\right]^{\frac{1}{30}} - 1\right)$$

(ii) annualized rates of return to physical capital

$$\left(\left[1+\alpha k_t^{\alpha-1}-\delta\right]^{\frac{1}{30}} - 1\right),$$

allowing the following period-by-period growth path comparisons to be made.

	Growth Rates (%)			
α = 1/3	2.97	1.52	1.04	0.87
α = 2/3	2.13	1.68	1.39	1.19

	Rates of Return (%)				
α = 1/3	14.0	9.3	7.8	7.3	7.1
α = 2/3	9.1	8.4	7.9	7.6	7.4

There is much less of a downward trend in both simulated paths, improving the historical accuracy.

Take-away: A higher value of α improves the model's prediction about historical growth, but how does one justify a higher value for the exponent on private capital? By introducing public capital as indicated in equation (3.14) from section 3.2.4.

6. Using the assumptions we have the following no-government transition equation
$$k_{t+1} = \frac{\beta}{1+\beta}(1-\alpha)Ak_t^\alpha = \frac{1}{3} \times \frac{2}{3} \times 10 \times k_t^{1/3} = 2.2222 k_t^{1/3}$$

(a) The steady state k with no government is
$$\bar{k} = (2.2222)^{3/2} = 3.3127.$$
In addition, $\bar{y} = A\bar{k}^\alpha = 10 \times 1.4907 = 14.907$, $\bar{w} = (1-\alpha)\bar{y} = 9.938$, and
$\bar{Y} = N\bar{y} = 100 \times 14.907 = 1490.7$.

(b) Introduce the government with $\varsigma = 0$, $c_t^g = 2$, and $k_0 = 3.3127$. Using (3.9) we can compute

$$k_1 = \frac{1}{3}\left[\frac{20}{3}(3.3127)^{1/3} - 2\right] = \frac{1}{3}[9.938 - 2] = 2.646$$

$$k_2 = \frac{1}{3}\left[6.6667(2.646)^{1/3} - 2\right] = 2.4069$$

$$k_3 = \frac{1}{3}\left[6.6667(2.4069)^{1/3} - 2\right] = 2.3114$$

$$k_4 = \frac{1}{3}\left[6.6667(2.3114)^{1/3} - 2\right] = 2.2714$$

$$k_5 = \frac{1}{3}\left[6.6667(2.2714)^{1/3} - 2\right] = 2.2544$$

Using the transition path for the capital-labor ratio, we can compute all related variables:
$w_0 = 9.938, w_1 = 9.221, w_2 = 8.934, w_3 = 8.814, w_4 = 8.763, w_5 = 8.741$
$y_0 = 14.907, y_1 = 13.831, y_2 = 13.401, y_3 = 13.221, y_4 = 13.145, y_5 = 13.112$
$Y_0 = 1490.7, Y_1 = 1383.1, Y_2 = 1340.1, Y_3 = 1322.1, Y_4 = 1314.5, Y_5 = 1311.2$. Note that under the assumptions of the problem, $\tau_t = \frac{c_t^g}{w_t} = \frac{2}{w_t}$, implying
$\tau_0 = 0.2012, \tau_1 = 0.2169, \tau_2 = 0.2239, \tau_3 = 0.2269, \tau_4 = 0.2282, \tau_5 = 0.2288$.

The effect of introducing government consumption is depicted diagrammatically in the figure below. An increase in government consumption shifts the transition equation down, reducing growth and leading the economy to a lower steady state value of k.

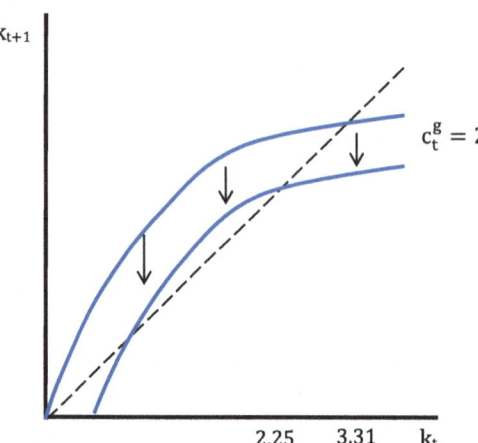

7. The transition equation where the only government purchase is public employment is identical to the no-government transition equation. In this case, the government does not alter aggregate saving because the wages taken from private sector workers are used to pay public sector workers who save at the same rate. The values of k_t, w_t, and y_t are unchanged. However, there are now 10 government workers to consider. Output per worker in the total workforce is now $Y_t/110 = 13.552$. The tax rate is $\tau_t = \varsigma/(1+\varsigma) = 0.0909$.

8. First, note that the constant coefficient, κ, before the expression involving k_t on the RHS of (3.14) is

$\frac{2}{3} \times 10 \times \left(\frac{1}{3}\right)^{7/9} \times (1-\tau)^{7/9} \times \tau^{2/9} = 2.8365 \times (1-\tau)^{0.7778} \tau^{0.2222}$. This expression can be used in *Problems* 8-10, where the only difference will be the value of τ. Here, $\tau = 0.10$ and the coefficient is $2.8365 \times 0.5523 = 1.5666$. The transition path is

$k_1 = 1.5666 \times (0.05)^{0.5555} = 0.2966$, $k_2 = 1.5666 \times (0.2966)^{0.5555} = 0.7976$, $k_3 = 1.3817$, $k_4 = 1.8748$, $k_5 = 2.2212$. For the steady state, $\bar{k} = (1.5666)^{2.2497} = 2.7453$.

9. For $\tau = 0.20$, the coefficient is 1.6676. The transition path is

$k_1 = 1.6676 \times (0.05)^{0.5555} = 0.3158$, $k_2 = 0.8790$, $k_3 = 1.5523$, $k_4 = 2.1290$, $k_5 = 2.5374$. For the steady state, $\bar{k} = (1.6676)^{2.2497} = 3.1597$.

10. For $\tau = 0.30$, the coefficient is 1.6446. The transition path is then $k_1 = 1.6446 \times (0.05)^{0.5555} = 0.3114$, $k_2 = 0.8602$, $k_3 = 1.5126$, $k_4 = 2.0697$, $k_5 = 2.4635$. For the steady state, $\bar{k} = (1.6446)^{2.2497} = 3.0629$.

The figure below depicts the transition equation for the three different tax rates.

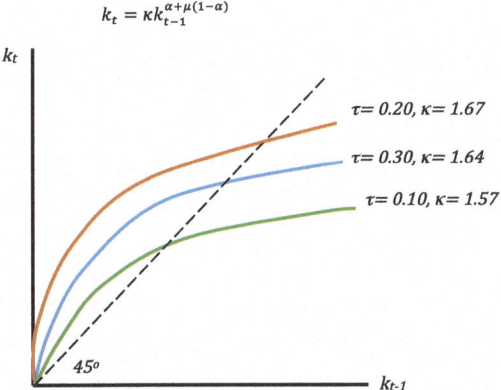

Remember from *Problem* 4 and the discussion in the text, the tax rate that maximizes the transition coefficient, or the height of the transition equation, is $\tau_t = \tau = \mu(1-\alpha)$, which here is 2/9 = 0.2222. As τ increases from 0.10 to 0.20, the coefficient increases because the coefficient maximizing τ has not yet been reached. However, as τ increases from 0.20 to 0.30, the coefficient maximizing τ has been surpassed. For τ greater than 0.2222, the coefficient is falling in τ.

11. If the exponent on the current capital stock is less than one there will be diminishing returns to capital accumulation that cause at least some decline in predicted growth rates. To prevent a decline in predicted growth rates, the transition equation would have to shift up over time. This could happen if the rate of private or public investment rose as a fraction of the economy's income. Higher rates of investment help offset the diminishing returns to a given unit of investment. There is evidence that the fraction of GDP devoted to public infrastructure, public education, and government support for R&D rose over much of the 20th century for many countries.

You can see this in our model by comparing *Problems* 8 and 9. Across these two problems there is an increase in the wage tax used to finance government investment that causes an upward shift in the transition equation, helping to maintain growth despite diminishing returns. However, this can't go on forever because public capital accumulation is also subject to diminishing returns and taxes eventually reduce private capital (compare *Problems* 9 and 10).

12.-13. Follow the detailed steps provided in the statement of the question from the text.

14. For $\varsigma = 0$, $\beta = 1/2$, and $\alpha = \mu = 1/3$,

$$\tau^{***} = \frac{0.2222}{0.5555} = 0.4000$$

$$\tau^{**} = 0.2222 \times \frac{1.5000}{1+0.50(0.5555)} = 0.2608$$

$\tau^* = 0.2222$.

15. Using the transition path from *Problem* 13 of Chapter 2 and the growth rate formula yields the following path of growth rates during the transition. Over the first two periods we have

$$\left[\left(\frac{0.8187}{0.05}\right)^{1/3}\right]^{1/30} - 1 = \left(\frac{0.8187}{0.05}\right)^{0.0111} - 1 = 3.15\%.$$ Over subsequent periods the growth rates are 1.04%, 0.35%, 0.11%, 0.04%.

In *Problem* 9 with public capital and $\alpha = \mu = 1/3$, we get the growth rates

$$\left[\left(\frac{0.3158}{0.05}\right)^{0.5555}\right]^{1/30} - 1 = \left(\frac{0.3158}{0.05}\right)^{0.0185} - 1 = 3.47\%.$$ Over subsequent periods the growth rates are 1.91%, 1.06%, 0.59%, 0.35%.

With public capital, the growth rates do not fall off as much and remain much higher, especially in the initial century of growth. If μ was higher there would be even less decline in the growth rates. However, some decline would remain, which is why it is important to include the rising rate of time investment in human capital, as we did in Chapter 2 and the rising rate of investment in public capital in this chapter.

16. $\bar{A}^B / \bar{A}^A = \left(N^B / N^A\right)^{(1-\xi)\mu} = 2^{2/9} = 1.17$. So, workers in location B are 17 percent more productive because the total public capital stock there is larger and there is impure sharing of its productive services.

17. Assuming $\mu = \alpha = 1/2$, (31) becomes $k_t = \left[\frac{Ag_t^{1/4}}{2r^*}\right]^2 = \frac{A^2 g_t^{1/2}}{4(r^*)^2}$. We also have

$y_t = AE_t g_t^{\mu(1-\alpha)} k_t^{\alpha} = AE_t g_t^{\mu/2} \left[\frac{Ag_t^{1/2}}{2r^*}\right] = \frac{A^2 E_t g_t^{1/2}}{2r^*}$.

(a) If A doubles, k_t and y_t each quadruple.

(b) If g doubles, k_t and y_t each increase by the factor $\sqrt{2}$.

(c) If r^* doubles, k_t falls to ¼ its initial value and y_t falls in half.

18. The open economy capital market equilibrium condition now becomes, $r^* = (1-\tau_t)\alpha AK_t^{\alpha-1}(E_t N)^{1-\alpha} g_t^{\mu(1-\alpha)} = (1-\tau_t)\alpha Ak_t^{\alpha-1} g_t^{\mu(1-\alpha)}$. Solving for the capital-labor ratio gives $k_t = \left[(1-\tau_t)\alpha Ag_t^{\mu(1-\alpha)}/r^*\right]^{\frac{1}{1-\alpha}}$. An increase in the tax rate now lowers the after-tax return to capital and causes a flight of capital from the country until the domestic return rises back to r^*.

19. See *Problem 1*.

20. See *Problem 8* from Chapter 2 and use the procedure described in deriving equation (8) from that chapter. The approach is the same.

21. Dividing (3.27b) by (3.27c) gives $\dfrac{g_{t+1}}{k_{t+1}} = \dfrac{\mu(1+\beta)}{1-\tau}$. The steady state version of this expression is (3.29a). In the steady state, (3.28) can be written as $\bar{k} = \kappa \bar{k}^{\alpha+\mu(1-\alpha)}$. Solving for $\bar{k}$ yields (3.29b). Given the production function for y_t, we can write the following steady state expression, $y_t = AE_t \bar{k}^\alpha \left(\dfrac{\mu(1+\beta)}{1-\tau}\bar{k}\right)^{\mu(1-\alpha)} = AE_t \bar{k}^{\alpha+\mu(1-\alpha)}[\mu(1+\beta)]^{\mu(1-\alpha)}(1-\tau)^{-\mu(1-\alpha)}$.

Substitute for $\bar{k}$ from (3.29b) in the steady state expression for y_t and then pull out the expressions involving $1-\tau$ and combine with $(1-\tau)^{-\mu(1-\alpha)}$ to get $(1-\tau)^{\frac{\alpha}{1-\alpha-\mu(1-\alpha)}}$. Carefully combine the remaining expressions and define them as Ω to get (3.29c).

22. Differentiate τ with respect to ϕ to get $\dfrac{d\tau}{d\phi} = -\dfrac{2[1-\beta(\alpha+\mu(1-\alpha))]}{(1+2\phi)^2} < 0$.

23. (a) Using (3.30), $\ln 2 = \dfrac{1/3}{(2/3)(1-\mu)} \times \ln 1.3077$, so $\mu = 0.8064$

(b) $y^R/y^P = 2 \times \dfrac{0.85}{0.65} = 2.6154$

24. (a) For the one period when aid flows in, we have $\frac{g_{t+1}}{k_{t+1}} = \frac{\mu(1+\beta)(1+\Delta)}{1-\tau}$. Substituting in (3.28) we have $k_{t+1} = \kappa(1+\Delta)^{\mu(1-\alpha)} k_t^{\alpha+\mu(1-\alpha)}$.

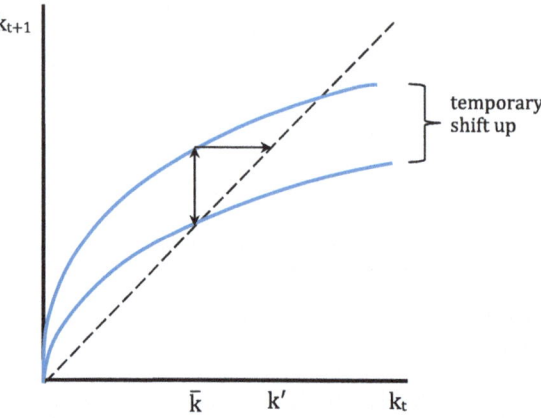

(b) Temporary aid in period t, shifts the transition equation up for one period. If you imagine starting in a steady state with $k_t = k_{t+1} = \overline{k}$, the new value for k_{t+1} will exceed the original value for $\overline{k}$. However, after the first period, the transition equation shifts back to its original position. This means the new value for k_{t+1} is unsustainable. Capital will fall back to the original steady state value over time.

Chapter 4
Schooling and Fertility

Reader's Guide

Section 4.1-4.2   Quantity and Quality of Children

Purpose: Our previous analysis tells us that human capital and population growth are both important determinants of the growth in worker productivity. However, up to this point, both have been treated as exogenous variables. This chapter will develop a theory of schooling and fertility.

Sticking Points: *(i)* The optimal fertility and schooling equations, (4.3a) and (4.3b), are somewhat complex. Part of the complexity is the new notation. The first thing you should do is to get comfortable with each new variable introduced in section 4.1.1. Make a "new vocabulary" list. After doing this, you can think about the meaning of the optimal choices.
        (ii) Fertility Start with the first equality of (4.3a). It takes the standard form of a demand equation for any good. Demand equations often have the form, income (adult potential income, $w_t D_t h_t$) divided by the price (net cost of raising a child, $\eta w_t D_t h_t - w_t D_t (T - e_t) \gamma \bar{h}$) of what is being demanded, which here defines the real income available to parents that can be spent on children (n_{t+1}). The optimal fraction of the real income that is spent on children depends on preferences, just as in any household demand theory. The relative strength of parents' preference for children, as opposed to consumption of goods, is given by $\dfrac{\psi}{1+\beta+\psi}$.

    The second equality of (4.3a) algebraically simplifies the expression to identify the variables that matter most and their effects on fertility. This simplification is literally the "bottom line" of the theory and makes analysis easier but it is hard to interpret without understanding the first equality. Besides preferences, there are two variables of the bottom line that matter: the relative productivity of children (γ) and the education of parents (e_{t-1}). A higher value for γ lowers the net cost of children because they are good little workers that bring income to the family which increases fertility. A higher value for e_{t-1} raises the opportunity of cost of taking time away from parental work to birth and raise young children which decreases fertility.
        (iii) Schooling Equation (4.3b) is even more complicated than (4.3a) because it accounts for a minimum amount of schooling that children must receive ($\bar{e}$) either because of government mandates about compulsory schooling/child labor or because very young children are simply not productive as workers but can begin learning. The notation "max [*x*, *y*]" means "take the bigger of *x* and *y*." In our theory *x* is the amount of schooling the parents *would like*

children to have if they were unconstrained by government mandates or by the lack of productivity of very young children. It is quite possible that this desired amount is less than y, which in our theory is $\bar{e}$. So, the parents don't get to *choose* schooling levels until the schooling that they desire for their children exceeds $\bar{e}$. When parents want their children to get more than the minimum schooling then $x > y$ and we can just focus on x, i.e. the awkward max $[x, y]$ notation can be ignored.

The optimal or desired amount of schooling depends, in part, on the effect of schooling in generating human capital and adult worker productivity which is captured by the expression $\frac{\theta}{1-\theta}$ (θ is the exponent on the schooling input in the human capital production function, $h_t = e_{t-1}^{\theta}$). This productivity expression is multiplied by the ratio of a measure of the net cost of raising children ($\eta w_t D_t h_t - w_t D_t T \gamma \bar{h}$) and the opportunity cost of sending older children to school rather than work ($w_t D_t \gamma \bar{h}$). The more expensive children are, the fewer parents will have but the children they do have will receive more schooling. The more productive older children are in generating family income, the higher is the cost of schooling and the less schooling they receive.

Doing the algebra that moves us to the second equality in (4.3b) again reveals which variables matter most and how they affect schooling. Apart from the productivity parameter θ, we get the same two variables that matter for fertility: the relative productivity of children (γ) and the education of parents (e_{t-1}). A higher value for γ raises the opportunity cost of sending children to school, which lowers schooling. A higher value for e_{t-1} raises the opportunity of cost of taking time away from parental work to birth and raise young children which decreases fertility but encourages parents to allow their fewer children to receive more schooling.

	Determinants			
	γ	e_{t-1}	e_t	$w_t D_t h_t$
n_{t+1}	+	−	−	0
e_t	−	+		0

(iv) Note the possible confusion between θ and γ because they both relate to some type of "productivity." The parameter θ determines the productivity of *schooling* in creating *adult human capital* and subsequently creating greater adult productivity at work. The parameter γ determines the *relative* productivity of an older child at *work* compared to an adult doing the same work with the same human capital from schooling (for example, when both the older child and adult have only the minimum amount of schooling).

Schooling and Fertility

Take Away: According to our theory when parents mull over their family plans they think about the costs of having children and the cost of sending them to school. Higher relative productivity of children and low parent education create incentives for parents to have more children with less schooling—the "quantity versus quality" of children tradeoff.

Sections 4.3-4.4   Schooling Dynamics

Purpose: Develop a transition equation for schooling, i.e. an equation that tells the value of e_t given the value of e_{t-1}.

Sticking Points The schooling transition equation is similar to the one for k_t but is more complex for the following reasons.

(i) The schooling transition equation must incorporate the minimum level of schooling, $\bar{e}$. This creates an interesting *low-schooling* steady state possibility. Fig 4.4 and the Numerical Example 4.4 illustrate a situation where there is only one other steady state, with *high-schooling*, that is very much like the steady state we focus on for k_t.

(ii) The transition equation for schooling can become even more complex when conditions place the transition equation in a position lower than the equation displayed in Fig 4.4. Look at Fig 4.3. Instead of two, there are now *three* steady state possibilities with low, intermediate, and high schooling. However, the intermediate steady state is *not* dynamically stable—if schooling is near it, schooling will either decrease toward the low steady state (when to the left of the intermediate steady state) or increase toward the high steady state (when to the right of the intermediate steady state).

Take-Away: The transition equation for schooling has three important implications.
(i) there might be one, two, or three steady states depending on the height of the transition equation
(ii) it is relatively easy for an economy to get trapped in a low-schooling steady state (low θ and e_{t-1} or high γ)
(iii) if an economy escapes the low schooling steady state, schooling will increase and cause worker productivity to grow in a manner similar to the growth in worker productivity caused by an increase in k_t
(iv) once schooling increases, fertility will begin falling and this will make it easier to accumulate physical capital per worker, further promoting gains in living standards

Section 4.5   The Schooling Poverty Trap

Purpose: Understand why economies get stuck in the low-schooling poverty trap

Sticking Points: The mathematical logic embedded in the form of the schooling transition equation tells us that the low-schooling steady state is more likely when the "initial" level of schooling (e_{t-1}) is low and when the relative productivity of children (γ) is high or the productivity of schooling is low (θ)—both of which shift the transition equation down and increases the range of e_{t-1} values that are "low"—i.e. that will track toward the low steady state. So what intuition do we attach to this logic about when countries find themselves in the poverty trap?

(i) Initial e_{t-1} can be low in countries where noneconomic reasons that we refer to as "cultural," create a weak demand for schooling.

(ii) The relative productivity parameter γ is often high in warmer climate that do "light" farming that does not require a lot of physical strength.

(iii) The schooling productivity parameter θ is low if either schools are poorly run or the state of technology in the country does not require schooling for workers to be productive.

Take-Away   Low-schooling poverty traps are a common reason for low living standards. To get out of this bad steady state requires some government policy intervention.

Section 4.6.1   *Malthus: The Traditional Economy*

Purpose: We have seen what an economy looks like in a low-schooling poverty trap. Before a country industrializes, it not only has low human capital but low physical capital as well. This is the world before the Industrial Revolution as described by Malthus's model of a *traditional economy* that does not rely on human and physical capital for production.

Sticking Points   There are two distinguishing characteristics of a traditional economy

(i) The two key inputs to production are not human and physical capital but rather are raw labor (N) and land or natural resources (L). The role of land is like physical capital except that it is not manmade and cannot be augmented.

(ii) Incomes are so low that consumption is close to the subsistence level. This is modeled by utility being expressed a function of the *difference* between actual consumption (c_t) and the subsistence level needed for survival (c).

Take-Away   Why go back to the pre-industrial world before 1800? Beyond historical interest, we do so because for many developing countries the Industrial Revolution didn't start until the second half of the 20th century (which is a big reason why they are relatively poor today) and because in many developing countries there is a "dual" structure where rural regions, or informal sectors of urban areas, continue to operate as traditional economies (even true in a middle-income country like China)

Section 4.6.2 Malthus: Fertility-Income Dynamics

Purpose: To explain why living standards show no upward trend in pre-industrial economies

Sticking Points: The Malthusian model is captured by two related figures (Fig.4.6 and Fig. 4.7).

(i) Fig. 4.6 is a production function relationship that says worker productivity (y) and the number of workers (N) are inversely related (based on equation (4.9′)). This is because of diminishing returns—when more workers try to farm a fixed amount of land, crowding occurs that lowers productivity.

(ii) Figure 4.7 is a plot of the positive effect of income on fertility (based on equation (4.15b)). As incomes rise and consumption pulls away from the subsistence constraint, parents feel like they can afford to have more children.
Many of the assigned Exercises involve using these two figures to analyze changing conditions in a traditional economy.

Take-Away: The key result of the model explains stagnant living standards. Positive productivity shocks occurred in traditional economies as people figured out better ways to farm. This caused a rise in income. The rise in income encouraged parents to have more children, which increased the population of future farmers. The increase in farmers crowded the land and lowered productivity back down to its original level. Positive productivity shocks ultimately allowed the economy to carry more people but income per person was unchanged.

Sections 4.7-4.10 Additional Topics

Purpose: Brief introduction to 5 topics related to the quantity-quality of children and Malthusian theories

Topics (i) *Escaping the Poverty* Trap—A country is stuck in a poverty trap because of overreliance on traditional production and child labor. Breaking out of traditional production requires sufficient technical progress and government policy support that allows modern firms driven by manmade physical capital to enter and make profit (see Chapter 6 for the details). Technical progress, causing an increase in θ, and government policy, child labor and compulsory schooling laws, can also break the economy out of the low schooling steady state. Today, government policy has to lead the way out of poverty traps because profitable modern technologies do exist but are underutilized.

(ii) *Fertility in Early Development*—Fertility tends to rise first, before falling, as economies begin to develop. There are two reasons for this. First, in northern climates, the shift away from "heavy" farming toward production in factories can raise the relative productivity of children and lower their net cost. Second, sustained increases in income lower the importance of the subsistence constraint, allowing a greater fraction of family resources to be devoted to raising children.

(iii) *Baby Boom*—The long, more than two-century, decline in fertility of advanced countries was interrupted by a temporary increase in fertility during the 20 years after WWII (especially in the US). One explanation is that older woman entered the work force to help keep production going during the war. The older woman tended to stay in the workforce after the war, thereby decreasing job opportunities for young women. Young women facing lower market wages decided to get married earlier and as a result had larger families over their child-bearing years.

(iv) *One Child Policy*—In the 1970s, China had the idea of mandating that each family be restricted to having at most one child. This caused a sharp decline in their fertility rate from about 3 children to 1. One possible benefit of the policy is to raise the schooling that the family's only child receives. However, the empirical evidence on this prediction is mixed.

(v) *Inequality*—Inequality of wages is a major issue in the US today. Wage inequality has been rising since 1980 and is due to a demand for college-educated workers that has grown faster than the supply (the fraction of the US workforce with a college degree has not increased much for 50 years). As a result, wages for educated workers has been rising faster than for those without a 4-year college degree. The inability of advanced countries to push larger fractions of its workforce through college and the resulting rise in wage inequality is becoming a common characteristic of advanced development.

Solutions to Exercises

Questions

1. Adult wages are $w_t D_t h_t$ and the wages of a child are $w_t D_t \gamma \bar{h} (T - e_t)$. Children earn less for three reasons: (i) less schooling ($\bar{h} \leq h_t$), (ii) lower productivity ($\gamma < 1$), (iii) fewer hours worked ($T - e_t < 1$).

2. Parents must simultaneously decide on the "quantity" (number) and "quality" (schooling time) of children. If children are relatively cheap, a low opportunity cost of raising them and a relatively high productivity of child labor, then parents will have more children and keep the schooling of each child low.

3. (a) Higher income resulting from greater parent's education relative to their older children, increases the opportunity cost of taking time to raise children and lowers the importance of child labor. This raises the net cost of children, so parents have fewer children but increase the schooling of the children they do have.

Schooling and Fertility

(b) The higher is the relative productivity of children, the lower is their net cost. A low net cost means parents will have more children and provide less education per child.

4. An increase in schooling of older children lowers their work and increases the net cost of children, causing fertility to fall. When the older children become adults they will have more human capital and earnings which increases the opportunity cost of raising children, causing fertility to fall in the next generation as well.

5. What causes fertility to change is a change in schooling. If schooling is stuck, so is fertility. Rising schooling causes fertility to decline.

6. As the schooling equation demonstrates, once conditions are met to escape the schooling trap, a dynamic occurs that causes schooling to increase and child labor to fall over time. There are various ways that this dynamic might begin, but once it does, the rise in schooling makes children increasingly more expensive (higher opportunity cost to raise children and less family income from children working). As a result, parents have fewer, but more educated, children as time passes.

7. An increase in the rental rate paid for a unit of human capital changes neither schooling nor fertility. Schooling does not change because a higher rental rate increases both parental income (which raises schooling) and the opportunity cost of children's schooling because they also receive higher pay (which lowers schooling). In our model these two conflicting effects exactly offset leaving schooling unaffected. Fertility does not change because schooling is unaffected.

8. Our model abstracts from many differences in households at the micro-level, instead focusing on the behavior of an *average* household over the course of development. The preference for children, and land holdings that generate non-labor income (see Chapter 7), vary across households within an economy causing variation in the number of children each household has. In the model of this chapter any variation in ψ, while affecting household fertility, does not alter schooling. Consistent with many statistical studies using household-level data, there can be variation in the quantity of children *without* variation in the quality of children. This does not contradict the fact that a rise in schooling in the economy as a whole is the key factor driving down fertility for the *average* household. The quantity-quality trade-off is more transparent in economy-wide averages that change over time, as rising schooling *causes* fertility to decline.

9. An increase in γ shifts the schooling equation down—from the one depicted in Figure 4 to the one depicted in Figure 3. To escape the schooling poverty trap, with a higher value for γ, the parent's education must exceed $\bar{e}$ by a greater amount– making the trap more likely.

10. Use Figure 4 and start with $e_0 > \bar{e}$.

11. (a) Culture can affect the importance a society places on schooling. For example, Protestants believe people need to find God on their own by reading the bible. This means at very early stages of development, children must receive enough schooling to make them quite literate (the bible isn't easy to read). So, a country such as the U.S., founded by those looking for the freedom to practice the Protestant religion, started with unusually high levels of education that enabled them to avoid the schooling-poverty trap.

(b) Technologies can affect the relative productivity of children. If production technologies raise the relative productivity of children, it raises fertility and lowers schooling. A good example is the "cottage" industry—the leading technology at the first stages of the Industrial Revolution in England. The production of cloth using child labor kept the level of fertility high and schooling low.

(c) Geography affects the relative productivity of children in agriculture. Harvesting southern crops (cotton, rice, sugar) is less physically demanding than northern crops (corn and wheat)—causing children growing up in southern regions to be more productive than those from northern regions. This is one reason education in the U.S. South lagged education in the U.S. North and Midwest.

12. (a)-(b) Compulsory schooling and child labor laws essentially do the same thing—they mandate that children must work less and go to school more. While this is one way to force an economy out of the schooling trap, it often does not work. Parents will not want to follow the law and unless they are closely monitored, they will keep their children working. Monitoring the family is particularly difficult in rural areas.

(b) Progresa-style family subsidies create an incentive for parents' to *willingly* send their children to school. The subsidy covers some fraction of the forgone wages associated with older children attending school, lowering the opportunity cost of education.

13. The period from the beginning of human history to around 1800 (the pre-industrial period), where there was little progress in living standards and modest increases in population size.

14. In a traditional economy the most important inputs complementing work effort are land and natural resources, where in a modern economy workers use large and sophisticated plant and equipment. In addition, consumption levels are close to subsistence.

15. As in a modern economy, fertility is negatively related to the cost of children. However, in addition, fertility increases with income as the subsistence constraint becomes less important.

16. The first component is $(4.9')$, the production function written on a per worker basis, that says a larger population reduces land per worker and worker productivity (the top figure in the diagram of the Malthusian model). The second component is $(4.15b)$, the fertility equation, that

Schooling and Fertility

says a rise in income relieves the subsistence constraint and increases the demand for children (the bottom figure in the diagram of the Malthusian model).

17. Remember where the two components of the Malthusian model come from. Figure 6 is a sketch of (4.9′) and Figure 7 is a sketch of (4.15b). Use these equations to guide your answers about slopes and shifts in the figures. The slope of Figure 6 is negative because higher values of N lower the land-labor ratio and reduce y. The slope pf Figure 7 is positive because higher income lessens the importance of the subsistence constraint and raises the demand for children.
(a) An increase in c has no effect on Figure 6 but Figure 7 shifts to the right and down (less fertility for any given level of income)
(b) An increase in L shifts Figure 6 to the right and up (workers are more productive with more land) but has no effect on Figure 7.
(c) An increase in A shifts Figure 6 to the right and up (increased knowledge about production make workers more productive) but has no effect on Figure 7.

18. Be able to reproduce and explain Figure 9 as discussed in the text, the most important result of this section.

19. Look at Figure 8 and start at the steady state, $\bar{N}, \bar{y}$. Now imagine the Black Plague reduces the population from $\bar{N}$ to N_0. The decrease in N causes y to increase to y_0. Now trace through the dynamics as the economy moves from N_0, y_0 back to $\bar{N}, \bar{y}$ as already depicted in Figure 8.

20. One possible explanation for the rise in fertility is a rise in the relative productivity of children as economies shift from (heavy) agricultural production to informal manufacturing production in the traditional sector and early factories in the modern sector. As the employment of children shifts from agriculture to domestic and formal industry, the relative productivity of children may rise. In our model this would be captured by a rise in γ. A rise in γ lowers the cost of children and increases fertility.

Another possible explanation for the early rise in fertility is related to the subsistence constraint. In the early stages of growth, before mandatory schooling and child labor laws, schooling may not rise above the education of young children. In the Malthusian model the importance of the subsistence constraint, c/y_t, falls with a rise with income. This lowers the value of forgone income associated with having and raising children, and increases fertility via an income effect. Thus, exogenous technological change that raises income will cause fertility to rise in the early stages of growth before schooling begins to increase.

21. The Baby Boom is the jump in U.S. fertility between 1945 and 1965. The entry of older women into the workforce during WWII depressed job opportunities and wages for young women after the war. Young women decided to marry and start their families earlier, resulting in more children.

22. An exogenous reduction in fertility both increases family resources and lowers the cost of schooling to the family, causing an increase in schooling. Recent empirical evidence for this result, in the context of China's one-child policy, is mixed.

In contrast to an exogenous change in fertility, *endogenous* variation in fertility, due to variation in the taste for children or in non-labor income, has no effect on schooling in our model. There is empirical evidence supporting this result. In our model, the quantity and quality of children are inversely related due to a strict *one-way* causation from schooling to fertility.

23. Technological progress and the growth in the high-skilled service sector in the later stages of development increases the demand for educated labor. Societies find it increasingly costly to raise the skills of students and to push larger fractions of the population through college. The supply of educated workers is unable to keep pace with the demand, resulting in an excess demand for highly educated labor. The excess demand raises the skill premium or the relative wage of workers with college degrees. In addition, years of schooling have risen for only a minority of the population causing a growing education gap between the highly educated and the majority with some college or less.

24. *G2* and *G3*—An important feature of development is the increase in schooling across generations. As each generation of parents become more educated (i) the relative importance of child labor decreases and (ii) the opportunity cost of raising children increases. As a result, parents increasingly choose to raise fewer children but to invest more in each child.

G7—Living standards remain stagnant in the traditional economies of the past because any gain in productivity causes income to rise above the subsistence level and increases the demand for children. The rise in fertility increases the population and lowers the land-labor ratio, offsetting the effect of new technology on worker productivity and wages. The dependence on land and the schooling trap must both be broken before living standards can take off.

Problems

1. Generate the first order conditions as indicated in the chapter appendix. Solve for schooling first. Assume that the strict equality holds in the first order condition for schooling. Divide the first order condition for schooling by the first order condition for fertility to get,

$$\frac{\theta}{e_t} = \frac{w_t D_t \gamma \overline{h}}{\eta w_t D_t h_t - (T - e_t) w_t D_t \gamma \overline{h}}.$$

Then solve the equation for e_t to get

$$e_t = \frac{\theta\left(\eta(e_{t-1}/\bar{e})^\theta - \gamma T\right)}{\gamma(1-\theta)}.$$

If this expression is greater than or equal to $\bar{e}$, then it is the optimal solution. If it is less than $\bar{e}$, then the constrained optimal solution is $\bar{e}$.

To solve for fertility, note that the first order condition for first period consumption gives us, $\lambda_t = 1/c_{1t}$. Using the first order condition for fertility, we can write

(i) $n_{t+1}\left(\eta w_t D_t h_t - (T - e_t) w_t D_t \gamma \bar{h}\right) = \psi c_{1t}$. Also, the first order condition for second period consumption gives us (ii) $c_{2t+1} = \beta R_t c_{1t}$. Substituting (i) and (ii) into the lifetime budget constraint and solving for first period consumption yields

$$c_{1t} = \frac{w_t D_t h_t}{1 + \beta + \psi}.$$

Substituting the solution for first period consumption into (i) and solving for fertility gives us (3a).

To solve for saving note that $c_{2t+1} = \beta R_t c_{1t} = R_t s_t$. Substituting $c_{1t} = \frac{w_t D_t h_t}{1 + \beta + \psi}$ and solving the second equality for s_t yields (3c).

2. The lifetime budget constraint becomes

$$c_{1t} + \frac{c_{2t+1}}{R_t} + n_{t+1}\eta w_t D_t h_t + n_{t+1} p_t x_t = w_t D_t h_t + n_{t+1} w_t D_t \gamma \bar{h}(T - e_t).$$ The first order conditions for schooling inputs, schooling time, and fertility are

(i) $\dfrac{\psi \theta_1}{x_t} = \lambda_t n_{t+1} p_t$

(ii) $\dfrac{\psi \theta_2}{e_t} = \lambda_t n_{t+1} w_t D_t \gamma \bar{h}$

(iii) $\dfrac{\psi}{n_{t+1}} = \lambda_t \left(\eta w_t D_t h_t - w_t D_t \gamma \bar{h}(T - e_t) + p_t x_t\right).$

Combining (i) and (ii), yields $x_t = \dfrac{\theta_1}{\theta_2} \dfrac{w_t D_t \gamma \bar{h}}{p_t} e_t$. Combining (ii) and (iii) as in *Problem* 1, and using the solution for goods inputs, gives us

$$e_t = \frac{\theta_2}{\gamma(1-\theta_1-\theta_2)} \frac{\eta\left(\frac{\theta_1}{\theta_2}\frac{w_{t-1}D_{t-1}}{p_{t-1}}\gamma\bar{h}\right)^{\theta_1} e_{t-1}^{\theta_1+\theta_2} - \gamma\bar{h}T}{\bar{h}}.$$

Now, low goods-input prices increase schooling investments in both goods and time. This means government subsidy of tuition costs associated with schooling inputs can help the economy escape the poverty trap associated with low schooling.

3. This problem completes the analysis in *Problem 2*. Substituting the solution for the schoolings goods input into the first order condition for fertility and into the lifetime budget constraint and then solving for fertility as in previous problems, gives

$$n_{t+1} = \frac{\psi}{1+\beta+\psi}\frac{1}{\eta-(T-(1+\theta_1/\theta_2)e_t)(\gamma\bar{h}/h_t)}.$$

The introduction of goods inputs associated with schooling will only affect fertility indirectly through its impact on schooling time and human capital accumulation.

4. There are studies indicating children's health affects their ability to learn and accumulate human capital (see Chapters 9 and 12). If this is the case, then important health investments in children can be modeled in the manner that we modeled school goods inputs. The trick in this modeling strategy is to obtain a reasonable estimate for θ_1 when x is interpreted as some composite of health investments in children. This is a potentially important extension of the analysis which could significantly improve our understanding of worker productivity.

5. (a) Solve the equation $0.1111 = \frac{\eta}{\gamma} - 0.5$, to get $\frac{\eta}{\gamma} = 0.6111$.

(b) If $\gamma = 0.30$, then $\frac{\eta}{0.30} = 0.6111$, or $\eta = 0.1833$.

(c) $e_t = 1.833\sqrt{e_{t-1}} - 0.5$

(d) $e_0 = 0.12, e_1 = 0.1351, e_2 = 0.1734, e_3 = 0.2634, e_4 = 0.4409, e_5 = 0.5000$

(e) see the figure below

Schooling and Fertility

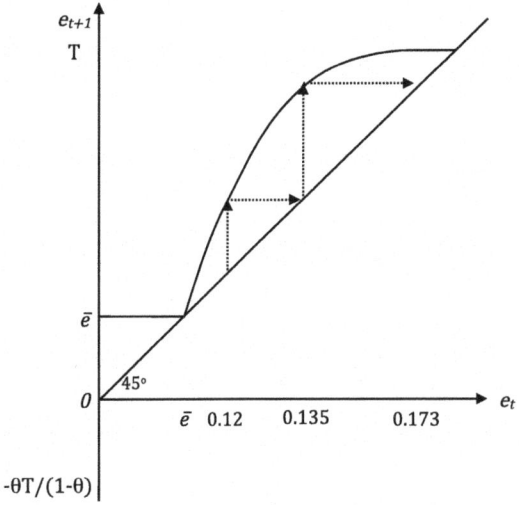

6. (a) $e_t = 1.5\sqrt{e_{t-1}} - 0.5$

   (b) $e_0 = 0.20, e_1 = 0.1708, e_2 = 0.1200, e_3 = 0.1111$
   (c) $\hat{e} = 0.25$

   (d) $e_0 = 0.30, e_1 = 0.32, e_2 = 0.35, e_3 = 0.39, e_4 = 0.43, e_5 = 0.49, e_6 = 0.50$

   (e) see the figure below

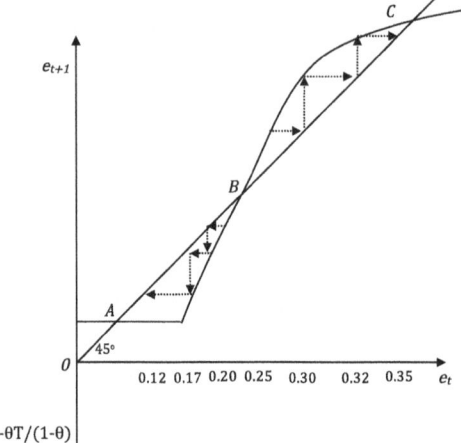

7. To proceed with the numerical example of the fertility path, start by defining $\tilde{\psi} \equiv \psi/(1+\beta+\psi)$ and use $\tilde{\psi}$ in equation (4.6)-(4.8). If $n_{t+1} = \frac{\tilde{\psi}}{\eta} = 1$, then $\tilde{\psi} = \eta = 0.1833$ (one needs a value for β to pin down ψ). The fertility gap across the two extreme cases is 2.75, so if there is 1 child per rich parent, there are 2.75 children per poor parent.

8. Take the schooling path from *Problem 5*. Starting in period 1 calculate the time path for the expression $\frac{0.5 - e_t}{\sqrt{e_{t-1}}}$: 1.053, 0.888, 0.568, 0.115, 0.000. Plugging these values into the fertility equation generates the fertility path of children per parent: 2.35, 1.94, 1.45, 1.07, 1.00.

9. From the text, we know that a Progresa subsidy effectively lowers the relative productivity of children, just as a reduction in γ would. A reduction in γ shifts the schooling transition equation up, reducing the likelihood of a schooling trap (similar to going from Figure 3 to Figure 4).

10. The total value of output must equal the total value of income as an accounting identity, $Y_t = w_t N_t + R_t^L L$. The identity can be written as $N_t y_t = N_t \left(w_t + R_t^L l_t \right)$. Dividing both sides of the identity by N_t and remembering that $y_t = Y_t / N_t = AL^\alpha N_t^{-\alpha} = Al_t^\alpha$, produces the result.

Schooling and Fertility

11. The first equality in (11) is true by definition; income not paid to workers must go to landowners. The second equality is obtained by pulling N_t out of both expressions in the difference. Finally, use (10) to establish the last equality. Equation (12) is obtained by dividing (11) by L.

12. Follow the chapter Appendix and fill in any missing details to get (15a) and (15b).

13. Using (15b), as income rises c/y_t falls and n_{t+1} rises. As $y_t \to \infty$, $c/y_t \to 0$ and n_{t+1} approaches its maximum value of $\dfrac{\psi}{1+\psi}\dfrac{1}{\bar{\eta}}$ which must exceed 1. In the steady state, n_{t+1} must be exactly 1 to keep the total population constant over time, $N_t = N_{t+1}$.

14. The steady state value of y_t is the income level that generates a constant population size, i.e. that generates $n_{t+1} = 1$. Using (15b), we have $1 = \dfrac{\psi}{1+\psi}\dfrac{1-c/\bar{y}}{\bar{\eta}}$. Solving for $\bar{y}$ yields $\bar{y} = \dfrac{c}{1-\dfrac{(1+\psi)\bar{\eta}}{\psi}}$. Note existence of a steady state requires $c > 0$ and $\dfrac{\psi}{1+\psi} > \bar{\eta}$.

15. Figure 8 displays dynamic stability whenever $y_0 > \bar{y}$. Use Figure 8 to show that $y_t \to \bar{y}$ when y is below $\bar{y}$. If y is below $\bar{y}$, then $N > \bar{N}$. In this situation, $n < 1$ and the population shrinks over time, causing y to rise to $\bar{y}$.

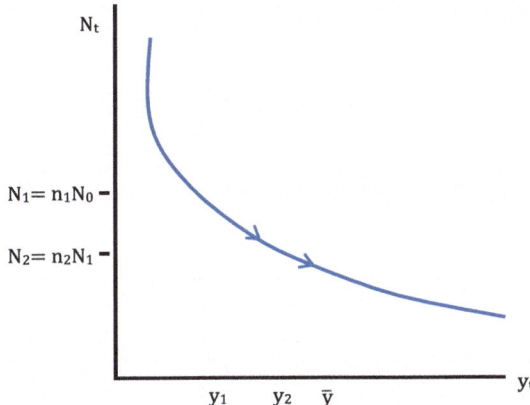

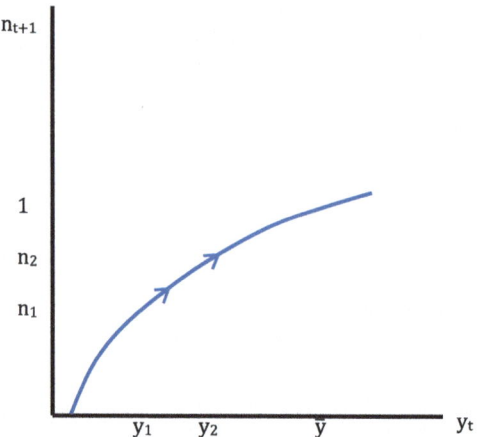

16. Taking fertility as given, the first order conditions for schooling and consumption are the same as before. However, to solve the household optimization problem, we now use the first order conditions to (i) express schooling in terms of consumption, (ii) solve for consumption in the budget constraint, and then (iii) substitute the solution for consumption back into the expression relating schooling and consumption to solve for the optimal schooling. The first order conditions for schooling and second period consumption yield $e_t = \psi \theta c_{1t} / n_{t+1} w_t D_t \gamma \bar{h}$ and $c_{2t+1} = \beta R_t c_{1t}$. Substituting into the budget constraint and solving for first period consumption gives $c_{1t} = \dfrac{w_t D_t h_t (1 - \eta n_{t+1}) + n_{t+1} w_t D_t \gamma \bar{h} T}{1 + \beta + \psi \theta}$. Substituting back in the first order condition for schooling gives $e_t = \dfrac{\psi \theta}{1 + \beta + \psi \theta} \left[\dfrac{h_t}{\gamma \bar{h} n_{t+1}} (1 - \eta n_{t+1}) + T \right]$, which is decreasing in fertility.

Chapter 5
A Complete One-Sector Model

Reader's Guide

Section 5.1.1-5.1.3   Private Sector

Purpose: Chapter 5 puts all the elements, covered in the text to this point, together in one model. The ultimate purpose is to explain large cross-country differences in living standards and then evaluate ways to reduce them. The first section looks at the private sector of the model.

Sticking Points: There is nothing new in the private sector of the model but it combines several features of past simpler models. The goal throughout the chapter is not to get lost in the details and complexity of a more complete model. Rather, you should review the analysis of the simpler models to gain an intuitive feel for what happens when everything is put together.

Take Away: Given the fiscal policy of the country, private households make important choices about fertility (n_{t+1}), schooling (e_t), and saving (s_t). The competition among private firms for productive inputs drives factor prices, r_t and w_t, to equal the marginal products of private capital and labor. The evolution of private capital intensity (k_{t+1}) is determined by household retirement saving and the effective labor supply, which depends on household fertility and schooling choices.

Section 5.1.4   Government Sector

Purpose: An important feature of the complete model is a theory of government behavior that makes fiscal policy endogenous (see section 3.6 of Chapter 3).

Sticking Points   (i) The government is characterized by the same variables as before. The difference is that the government now *chooses* c_t^g, g_{t+1}, and τ_t (government employment remains exogenous).
(ii) The government chooses fiscal policy to maximize a type of "grand" utility function that includes the benefits of government consumption (to the officials and their close supporters) as well as the lifetime utility of private sector households in the current and future generations. The government worries about the future and makes fiscal policy plans over an indefinite time horizon.
(iii) The key new parameter of the "grand" utility function is ϕ, the relative weight the government places on private household utility versus the utility generated

from government consumption. A more selfish/corrupt government is modeled as having a lower ϕ (it could even be zero)

(iv) A couple of points to note about the government's optimal solutions given by equations (5.10a) and (5.10b). The government saves and invests a *fixed share or fraction of national income* equal to $\beta\mu(1-\alpha)$. We can think of this fixed share as the product of taxes collected per dollar of national income (τ) times the fraction of tax revenue the government uses for investment (call it B, as we will do in a later section). Given that $\beta\mu(1-\alpha) = \tau \times B$, this means that τ and B are inversely related, as suggested in our main take-away below.

Take-Away: The income tax rate is a decreasing function of ϕ and the share of tax revenue that is invested in public capital rather than government consumption is an increasing function of ϕ. A more benevolent government taxes less and invests a larger share of tax revenue in the country's infrastructure.

Section 5.1.5   Steady State Equilibrium

Purpose: Understand the long-run or steady state position of an economy in the complete model. Determine why some countries generate a "rich"—high labor productivity steady state rather than a "poor"—low labor productivity steady state.

Sticking Points: There are two fundamental long-run drivers that determine a country's steady state position. The first is the *schooling poverty trap*. A rich country escapes the trap and a poor country does not. The second, and very much independent driver, is the *fiscal policy* of the country. If it is pro-growth (low taxes—high government investment) the country is richer in the long-run.

Take-Away An economy's steady state is determined by its (i) initial position with regards to schooling (e_t) and (ii) government's attention to private household welfare (ϕ).

Section 5.2   Cross-Country Income Differences

Purpose: Calibrate the complete one-sector growth model to see if it explains large gaps in worker productivity across countries.

Sticking Points: (i) The calibration uses estimates and empirical observations that are similar to those we used previously. One exception is the calibration of the parameter ϕ. We set the value of ϕ in the rich country to match government purchases as a share of GDP in the US and in the poor country to match the same fraction in a sample of poor countries with large

A Complete One-Sector Model

governments—see section 3.6 from Chapter 3. It is important to note that not *all* poor countries have large governments compared to the size of their economies, but some do.

(ii) The government purchase share of GDP is equivalent to the income tax rate in our model because we interpret the tax rate as being *net* of government transfers—such as Social Security, Medicare, and unemployment compensation. Transfer program in developed countries are relatively large, now making up more than half of all government spending. However, these programs essentially just shuffle income from one household to another and thus do not have the same effects as government purchases. See Chapter 11 for an analysis of government transfers.

(iii) The worker productivity gap between rich and poor countries in the model is quite large—close to those observed between the richest and poorest countries of the world. We use equation (5.11) to "decompose" the *sources* of the gap in Table 5.2. The decomposition is useful, but it should be noted that the decomposition underestimates the causal role of the schooling poverty trap. This is because lower human capital and high fertility negatively affect the growth of g_t and k_t, as you can see from the transition equations for each. Thus, some of the credit the decomposition gives to these physical capital stocks for explaining the gap is due to the indirect effects of differences in human capital.

Take-Away: The schooling poverty trap and the high tax-high consumption fiscal policy of the poor country significantly limit worker productivity and living standards. We next turn to identifying ways of alleviating a poor country's barriers to growth.

Our analysis ignores a major impediment to development: conflict. Many countries that remain poor do so because ethnic divisions cause political instability and civil war. See section 3.6.6 on Severe Government Failure. In this sense politics, and not economics alone, can be the most important reason for poverty.

Sections 5.3, 5.4.1   Foreign Aid

Purpose: To begin an assessment of programs and policy reforms designed to alleviate poverty. In this section we look at a simple benchmark approach—providing aid to bolster the government revenue of a poor country.

Sticking Points: (i) The idea of providing aid to a poor country's government is based on the hope that they will use the funds to carry out investments needed to jump-start growth. If there are no specific "springs attached" to how the funds are used, it is called *unconditional* aid or *budget support*.

(ii) When aid donors attach conditions on the use of funds, the aid is called *conditional*. However, in many cases, the donors are either unwilling or unable to track the exact use of funds. When this is true, conditional aid is essentially equivalent to unconditional aid.

(iii) The best way to think about the effects of unconditional aid is to imagine it as an increase in government revenue that causes a temporary upward shift in the transition equation for g_t. *Problem* 24 of Chapter 3 gives an explicit analysis supporting this interpretation. It does not change τ or B (which depend on the fundamental nature of governing officials as given by ϕ) but rather only the extra revenue available. The transition equation shifts up because some portion of the aid inflow will be invested (based on the value of ϕ).

(iv) When the aid is stopped, the transition equation for g_t shifts back down to its original position (where the tax base that funds investment is based on domestic income only). This implies the new higher level of g_t will be *above* the country's sustainable steady state value. So, g_t will fall, as will k_t since it depends on g_t (see 5.10c). The decline in g_t and k_t, as they return to their original steady state values, causes growth to fall below the steady state value of 1% per year.

Take-Away: Unconditional aid increases government revenue, only a portion of which is invested in public capital. Once the aid stops, because nothing has fundamentally changed about the country or its government, the economy returns to its original steady state. There is no long-run improvement in worker productivity and living standards. Disappointing growth outcomes associated with foreign aid have caused some analysts to focus more on promoting *remittances* from people who have migrated away from the developing country to richer countries. This notion links the world development strategy of richer countries to their immigration policies. We focus on capital flows across borders rather than labor flows.

Section 5.4.2   Opening the Economy

Purpose: To assess whether opening a developing country's borders to capital flows promotes economic growth.

Sticking Points: (i) The basic idea behind opening the economy is to use foreign saving to fund domestic private investments within the country. This is potentially quite beneficial to a poor country with little saving of its own.

(ii) The big catch is that a small private capital stock may not imply the high marginal product of capital needed to generate the high return on investment that attracts foreign funding. The poor country must have laid some groundwork for growth by having a reasonably well-educated workforce, decent infrastructure, and a pro-business policy stance.

(iii) An additional advantage to opening is that it forces the government to choose a new fiscal policy with lower tax rates and a higher fraction of revenue invested. This is because it is now competing for international capital with other countries.

(iv). There will be some domestic opposition to opening from a potentially powerful domestic interest group. The country's capital owners (the initial generation of households at the time of opening, generation-0 in the simulation) could see their return to capital fall if foreign capital flows into the country.

Take-Away: There is a major potential growth advantage to attracting foreign saving and private physical capital into a country. For example, the 19th century Industrial Revolution in the US would not have happened without capital inflows from England. However, to exploit this possibility, the country must be careful not to undermine the high returns that *should* result from a scarcity of private capital.

Section 5.4.3   *Eliminating the Poverty Trap*

Purpose: To devise policies that can effectively raise schooling.

Sticking Points: (i) Schools don't work like the baseball park in the movie *A Field of Dreams*—"if you build it, they will *not* necessarily come." This is because the most significant cost of school attendance to a family is the forgone wages of older children that have to give up work to attend school.

(ii) There are two strategies to increase school attendance once the schools are built. The most common one is to mandate attendance or equivalently to outlaw child labor. This strategy does not work well, especially in rural areas where laws cannot easily be monitored, because it is not in the parents' interest to send older children to school. A more effective strategy is to subsidize family income of attending students through compensation of at least some portion of the wages forgone from child labor.

(iii) A nice implication of schooling dynamics is that if the government can push education sufficiently higher, i.e. sufficiently above $\bar{e}$, no further subsidy will be required. Once parents are sufficiently well educated, they will choose to have fewer and better educated children without a subsidy.

(iv). A snag in the subsidy strategy is that the direct effect of the wage compensation also reduces the cost of having children, creating an incentive to have more children. The rise in schooling must be larger to offset this possible negative unintended consequence. In our simulation this is the case.

Take-Away: Perhaps the single most important growth-promoting policy is to create incentives for parents to increase the schooling of their children.

Section 5.4.4   *Fiscal Policy Reform and Aid*

Purpose: To examine a common approach to promoting growth, but one that is expensive to pull off.

Sticking Points: (i) Pro-growth fiscal reforms are often recommended or attached as conditions to aid. In our model, pro-growth reforms would be to lower taxes and invest a larger fraction of revenue in public infrastructure.

(ii) The snag in this approach is that it is not in the interest of the poor country's government to reform—they like the current fiscal policy just fine. To actually get them to reform would require enough of an "aid-bribe" to at least make them indifferent between the no aid-no reform equilibrium and the aid-reform equilibrium.

(iii) In our model, the amount of aid needed to make the government indifferent to reform is very high and it must last as long as the reforms stay in place.

Take-Away: In dealing with governments that are not pro-growth, there is little the outside world can reasonably do to reform fiscal policy.

Solutions to Exercises

Questions

1. The complete one sector model has three endogenous types of capital that complement work effort and raise worker productivity—private physical capital, public or government physical capital, and human capital. The model also includes endogenous fertility that determines population growth and the capital available per worker. Long-run differences in living standards across countries are due to a combination of (i) the schooling-fertility interaction and (ii) the endogenous choice of fiscal policy that determines how much private saving is reduced by taxation and how much tax revenue is invested by the government rather than consumed.

2. A higher private stock of physical capital increases income and the tax base. A fraction of the tax base is invested by the government. So, more private capital implies more public capital.

3. A recursive solution is one where the solution can be found step by step in a sequence of calculations. Most of the models in the book have a recursive structure with regard to the solving dynamic paths in the sense that the solutions for the endogenous variables do not need to be solved for simultaneously over the entire path all at once. For example, in Chapter 2 we could solve for the capital-labor ratio period by period, creating a sequence of solutions to generate a dynamic path. The model of this chapter is more complicated because we have four key endogenous variables. Fortunately, it is still true that the dynamic paths can be solved period by period in a time sequence. Furthermore, the model has a recursive structure *within* each time period that further simplifies the calculations.

The dynamic path of the economy is determined by the evolution of schooling (5.1b), fertility (5.1a), private capital (5.10c), and public capital (5.10b). However, we do not need to

A Complete One-Sector Model

solve these four equations simultaneously in each period of the transition. First, (5.1b) can be used to solve the entire dynamic path of schooling, independent of all other variables. Next, the dynamic path of schooling can be used to solve the entire dynamic path of fertility. Finally, using the paths of schooling and fertility, we can simultaneously solve (5.10b) and (5.10c) in each period to get the dynamic paths of private and public capital.

4. A more selfish government is captured by a weaker concern for private household utility, a lower value of ϕ. A lower value of ϕ translates into a higher tax rate. The higher tax rate reduces the after-tax wage rate and household saving. Less household saving results in less private capital accumulation. It is also important to note that while the selfish government collects more tax revenue, they invest a smaller fraction of it in public capital (any additional tax revenue collected is not invested but is rather consumed). The fraction of available national income that is invested by the government is, in fact, independent of ϕ. This also means that because there is less private capital accumulation and national income, there will be less public capital accumulation.

5. There are two fundamental differences between rich and poor countries that cause steady state differences in their worker productivity. The first difference is the level of schooling. The poor country is stuck in the poverty trap where only very young children receive schooling, while in the rich country children receive the maximum level of schooling. The schooling difference also leads to high fertility in the poor country and low fertility in the rich country. The second difference relates to the fiscal policies of the two countries. The rich country's government places greater weight on the welfare of the private citizens in choosing taxes and public investment. As a result, the rich country has a lower tax rate and a higher rate of public investment out of tax revenue. Both fundamental differences create differences in private capital accumulation per worker.

6. The weight placed on the welfare of private households is inversely related to the net tax rate set by the government officials. This allows us to use observations on net tax rates to calibrate the value for these weights. Many poor countries have high net tax rates, implying low weights placed on the welfare of private households.

7. Table 2 presents the steady state worker productivity ratio, across rich and poor countries, generated by the model. The features included in the model cause the rich country to be over 28 times richer than the poor country. The table provides a decomposition of the worker productivity ratio based on the following expression for worker productivity,

$$y_t = \frac{k_t^\alpha AE_t g_t^{\mu(1-\alpha)} \hat{h}_t}{1 + n_{t+1}(T - e_t)}.$$

The poverty trap causes the term $\hat{h}_t / (1 + n_{t+1}(T - e_t))$, average human capital per worker, to be 3.7 times higher in the rich country for two reasons. First, since $e_t = 0.5$ in the rich-equilibrium and $e_t = \bar{e} = 0.08$ in the poor-equilibrium, adult human capital differs across countries. This causes output per worker in the rich country relative to that in the poor country to be 2.10. Second, the high fertility in the poor country implies that their workforce contains a sizeable fraction of young workers, who are less productive than adult workers due to less strength and experience (captured by $\gamma = 0.28$). This causes worker productivity to be 1.75 times higher in the rich country. The role of worker-age in determining low worker productivity is overlooked in most studies.

The poverty trap also causes low values of k and g. High population growth increases the size of next period's workforce relative to the current period's savers. High population growth spreads saving and capital accumulation more thinly across workers in the future, lowering k. Lower values of k and $\hat{h}$ lower the tax base and reduce public investment for any given tax rate.

The lower value of ϕ in the poor country raises tax rates and further reduces private saving and private capital formation. Indirectly this also lowers public capital formation by reducing the level of national income and the tax base. These various effects that serve to lower public and private physical-capital intensities in the poor country cause worker productivity to be 7.7 times higher in the rich country.

8. The estimate for differences in adult human capital is close to that found in Hall and Jones (1999), although they use a different approach to estimation. The difference is worker productivity caused by physical capital intensity (both private and public) is four times larger than in Hall and Jones. There are several reasons for this. First, in Table 3 we are assuming that the poor country is a perfectly closed economy. An open economy reduces the differences in capital intensity across rich and poor countries, although not completely. The typical poor country is neither perfectly open nor perfectly closed, so our estimates using perfectly closed and perfectly open economies should bound the estimate from Hall and Jones.

Second, there are reasons to believe that the Hall and Jones estimates may be too low. Pritchett (2000) estimates that the actual capital stock in poor countries is between 57 and 75 percent of the officially measured capital stock. Thus, in poor countries the level of government consumption is under-estimated and the level of investment is over-estimated. This fact implies estimates of productivity differences that are based on direct estimates of capital stock differences, as in Hall and Jones, are too small.

Third, the Hall and Jones approach also treats private and public investment as perfect substitutes in production (we model the two inputs as distinct complements). The estimates of the output-elasticity of public capital, suggest that this is not the case; the elasticity for public capital is less than two thirds the elasticity for private capital (Glomm and Ravikumar (1997)). Poor countries have relatively more public capital, implying that the perfect-substitutes assumption overstates the productivity of the capital stock in poor countries and lowers the estimated role of capital differences in explaining worker productivity differences.

9. This question summarizes the reasons for the poverty trap from Chapter 4. Cultural differences create different noneconomic incentives for educating children. For example, in some versions of Christianity it is important for all individuals to read the bible. This creates a

A Complete One-Sector Model

cultural incentive for everyone to become literate, resulting in a higher level of schooling at low levels of development than would otherwise be the case. This makes it more likely that the country will escape the schooling poverty trap by making the "initial" values of adult education relatively high.

Geography and technology affect whether a country is in a poverty trap by affecting the relative productivity of children. A high relative productivity of children implies a higher level of parental education is required to escape the poverty trap. Geography affects the relative productivity of children because farming associated with warmer climates tends to be less physically demanding, which raises the relative productivity of young children. Technology raises the relative productivity of children when the technology used in production requires little training and physical strength. The cottage industry, during the Industrial Revolution in England, was able to use young children productively. This may explain the delay in schooling in England relative to other countries that began to experience modern growth.

Finally, θ may differ across countries, reflecting differences in the quality of schooling. In our numerical simulations, we assume the values for γ and θ are the same across rich and poor countries. Differences in schooling are due solely to differences in initial conditions.

10. Unconditional aid is a transfer of funds to the government with no strings attached. We can think of the government as an infinitely lived household. The unconditional aid is simply a temporary rise in budget income. The principle of consumption smoothing indicates that at least some of the temporary rise in income will be saved and invested by the government to allow income and consumption to rise in the future as well as in the current period. How much of the income is saved depends on the government's discount factor, β. The higher the discount factor the more temporary income will be saved.

In the policy simulation some of the aid is definitely invested in public capital. The investment in public capital raises the marginal product of human capital and wages, which causes an increase in private saving and private capital. These effects cause a modest rise in the economy's growth rate from period 1 to period 2.

However, the modest rise in the growth rate cannot be sustained for two reasons. First, even if the rise in saving and investment could be sustained, the growth rate will decline because of diminishing marginal productivity. Second, the rise in investment itself cannot be maintained because the rise in aid is only temporary. When the aid stops flowing, the economy cannot save enough to maintain the new higher capital stocks. Nothing fundamental has changed in the economy, which means it must return to the initial steady state. The aid pushes the economy beyond its steady state temporarily, but eventually the economy returns to its original position. This is why the growth rate eventually drops below the growth caused by exogenous technological change during the return to the original steady state.

11. In a perfectly open economy with no uncertainty, and thus no investment risk, the private after-tax marginal product is equalized across countries. This does not imply that k is equalized unless fiscal policy is identical across countries. A country with relatively high tax rates and relatively low levels of public capital will require smaller values of k to raise the marginal

product of capital enough to equalize the after-tax marginal product, as demonstrated in the figure below.

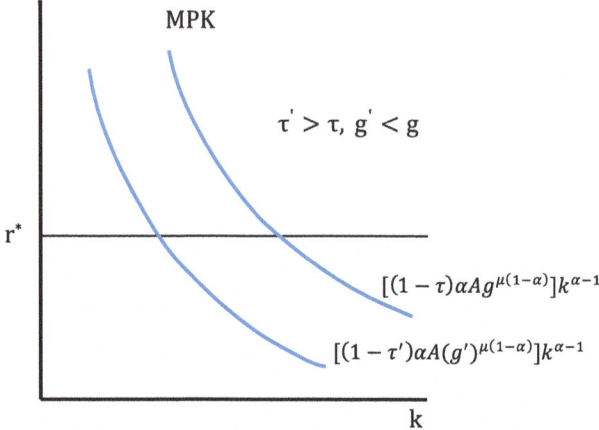

12. In an open economy the cost of taxation increases in *present value*. In a closed economy, taxes lower after-tax wages, saving, and ultimately capital accumulation in the *next* period. In an open economy, higher taxes cause existing capital to move to another country in the *same* period. The higher cost of taxation lowers the optimal tax rate.

The same type of argument applies to the public investment rate. In a closed economy, greater public investment raises wages, saving, and then private capital accumulation next period, which increases the private capital stock two periods from the public investment. In an open economy, greater public investment raises the public capital stock and the marginal product of private capital next period. This causes a private capital inflow next period, one period ahead of the private capital response in a closed economy. Thus, the optimal public investment rate out of tax revenue is higher in an open economy.

In short, an open economy causes private capital to respond more rapidly to fiscal policy.

13. The worker productivity gap shrinks from 28.3 to 8.98. This happens because the after-tax return to private capital is higher in the poor country, causing a capital inflow. The return is higher because the closed economy value of k is very low. The inflow of private capital is made greater by the pro-growth change in fiscal policy in the poor country, once it opens the economy, that raises the after tax return to private capital.

14. There are clear gains in worker productivity from opening the economy in the poor country. However, not all generations benefit from the opening. The policy affects the welfare of households by affecting factor prices. Households prefer higher current wages for themselves

A Complete One-Sector Model

and higher future wages for their children. They also benefit from higher interest rates on their life-cycle saving. Opening the economy will raise wages and lower interest rates as capital flows into the economy. For *most* generations there is a net gain in utility from these factor price adjustments (the effect of higher wages is greater than the effect of lower interest rates). This is *not* true for the initial generation of old households who are alive at the time the policy is introduced. Their current wages are unaffected by the capital inflows (since the initial steady state capital intensity is fixed) and yet their interest rates are significantly lowered. The sharp drop in interest rates, with no change in current wages, causes their welfare to fall. Thus, welfare falls for the initial old generation and rises for all others.

The government in the poor country enjoys an increase in public consumption each period—the increase in the tax base from capital inflows offsets the drop in tax rates. The utility gain from the rise in government consumption, along with the discounted gain in utility to all future generations, is larger than the loss in welfare of the initial generation. Thus, the poor government would want to open the economy, on economic grounds, in our setting.

15. The Progressa program subsidies the family for the earnings that are lost when their older children attend school instead of working. If the subsidy is sufficiently large, then the cost of sending older children to school becomes small enough to generate a rise in schooling and an escape from the trap. See Chapter 4 for more discussion,

16. Compulsory schooling, if it can be widely enforced (a potentially large "if"), is a policy that can push the economy out of the poverty trap. As with all policies that force private households to behave in ways that they would not have chosen, the initial generation of households will be made worse off. Thus, unlike the Progressa subsidy that rewards the household enough to voluntarily change its behavior, forced compulsory schooling will lower private welfare initially.

The government, however, prefers compulsory schooling for two reasons. First, it does not require a loss in revenue needed to finance the subsidy (again assuming the enforcement costs are not higher than the revenue saved on the subsidy). Second, the schooling subsidy also subsidizes fertility. Compulsory schooling will lower fertility relative to the subsidy.

17. The fiscal reform imposes a fiscal policy in the poor country that would bring it in line with the fiscal policy of the rich country. It imposes the τ and B of the rich country, where the optimal values are 0.15 and 0.67, on the poor country, where the corresponding optimal values in the open economy are 0.26 and 0.31.

The effect of fiscal policy reform on the growth rates of worker productivity is relatively modest and short-lived. In part, this is because we begin the policy experiment from a perfectly open economy. Opening the economy brings the fiscal policy of the poor government closer to that of the rich government (see Table 5.3). This has the effect of making the differences in tax policy less dramatic and the returns to accumulating private and public capital smaller (since capital intensities are higher in the open economy than in the closed economy). When the poor economy is relatively close to the rich country's capital intensities to begin with (see Table 5.4), the transition to new steady state is short.

There is, however, a significant gain in utility of all generations from the fiscal reform. This is because of the growth effects and because of the direct effects of paying lower taxes. Of course, the welfare of the poor country's government falls significantly since they have been moved off their optimal fiscal policy.

18. The aid costs of the policies we examined differ significantly. The unconditional aid policy comes at a price and delivers no long-term benefits. Openness and the Progresa-style education subsidy deliver large and sustained increases in income. They also increase the welfare of the poor country's government and thus should be readily accepted. However, openness hurts the initial generation of private households, and thus may not increase the government's welfare for all calibrations (for example, if the government's β is low). At a minimum, the government may use the fact that the current generation is hurt as a "bargaining chip" to induce some aid compensation for opening the economy. Strategic considerations also enter in the case of the Progresa program. The government prefers compulsory schooling, and they may use this as a threat point to induce aid compensation for going forth with the Progresa program.

Fiscal reforms would certainly be opposed by the poor country's government. Aid dollars would have to be used to "purchase" the fiscal reforms from the poor country's government, in compensation for its losses. The cost to maintain the reforms are large and permanent.

19. Our analysis is consistent with three possible reasons for the lack of correlation. First, unconditional aid, including aid where conditions are not adequately enforced, will not deliver long-term gains in income. The boost to growth from unconditional aid is short-lived and so modest that it could easily be overshadowed by other developments – e.g., any long-lasting effects of the negative shocks to the economy that initially triggered the scaling up of unconditional aid to begin with.

Second, while there are policies that can generate rapid growth and sustained increases in income, there is likely to be domestic conflict over which policy to pursue. The government favors opening the economy and compulsory schooling, but the current generation of private households will oppose both policies. The current generation of private households favors the Progresa program, a program which the government views as clearly inferior to compulsory schooling. These conflicts may undermine attempts to achieve domestic consensus on which growth-promoting and poverty-reducing policies to implement. Such lack of consensus could delay or undermine the negotiation and implementation of conditional aid agreements with donors.

Finally, our analysis suggests that reforms of domestic fiscal policy are likely to be the least successful of the policies that we examined. The growth effects of fiscal reform are relatively modest and short-lived and the aid-cost of "buying" the reforms from the poor country's government are enormous. Even if the aid is carried out in sufficient amounts

A Complete One-Sector Model

indefinitely, there will be little correlation between aid and economic growth in the data. The growth effects occur early on, while the aid continues into the future during periods where the growth effects have long since vanished.

20. Yes. There is evidence that food aid sent to countries experiencing internal conflict can prolong civil war. As is often quoted, "an army travels on its stomach," and much of the food aid is diverted to soldiers on both sides of the conflict. Civil wars hurt economic growth and humanitarian aid can prolong civil war.

21. This chapter shows a country with a selfish government and a schooling poverty trap will have dramatically lower worker productivity than a country with a pro-growth government and high schooling. Low schooling, high child labor and fertility, high taxes, and low public investment all serve to keep capital stocks per worker low (private and public physical capital, as well as the average human capital in the workforce). However, these features fall short of explaining the very largest income gaps observed across rich and poor countries. The second half of the book introduces a two-sector approach that includes additional features that help to explain high fertility, weak physical capital accumulation, and low worker productivity in poor countries during the earliest stages of development.

Problems

1. The procedure for finding the optimal household solutions is as in *Problem* 1 of Chapter 4.

2. Start with the capital market equilibrium condition, $K_{t+1} = s_t N_t$. Substituting the household saving expression from (5.1c) yields $K_{t+1} = \frac{\beta}{1+\beta+\psi}(1-\tau_t)w_t h_t D_t N_t$. Writing out the human capital rental from (5.4b), $K_{t+1} = \frac{\beta}{1+\beta+\psi}(1-\tau_t)(1-\alpha)AE_t g_t^{\mu(1-\alpha)} k_t^\alpha h_t N_t$. Now divide both sides of the equation by $E_{t+1}\hat{h}_{t+1}N_{t+1}$ to derive (5.6).

3. Unlike private households with finite lifetimes, the government has a less clear planning horizon because public officials are charged with considering how their actions affect the welfare of future generations. Equation (5.7) assumes the planning horizon of the government extends out to the indefinite future (an infinite number of periods). As for private households, (5.7) assumes public officials discount the future, placing a smaller weight, β^t, on members of generation-t than on the current generation of households. Government officials are also modelled as placing a different weight on the welfare of private households relative to their own welfare. The more altruistic the public official the larger the value of the parameter ϕ.

4. Carefully follow the detailed instructions given in the chapter Appendix to find the solution.

5. From Table 2 we know $\left(\frac{g^R}{g^P}\right)^{\mu(1-\alpha)} = 2.09$ and $\left(\frac{k^R}{k^P}\right)^{\alpha} = 3.68$. From (5.4a), we have

$$\frac{r^P}{r^R} = \left(\frac{g^P}{g^R}\right)^{\mu(1-\alpha)} \left(\frac{k^P}{k^R}\right)^{\alpha-1} = \frac{1}{\left(g^R/g^P\right)^{\mu(1-\alpha)}} \left(\frac{k^R}{k^P}\right)^{1-\alpha} = \frac{1}{2.09}\left(3.68^{1/\alpha}\right)^{1-\alpha} = \frac{13.5424}{2.09}$$

$= 6.4796$. Using the relationship between the returns across our periods and annualized returns found in real world data, we have $\dfrac{\left(1+r_a^P\right)^{20}-1}{\left(1+r_a^R\right)^{20}-1} = 6.4796$. If $r_a^R = 0.07$, then $r_a^P = 0.16$. For the marginal products to be more equal in our model, g^R/g^P must increase (perhaps because of corruption in the poor country—see Chapter 3) or k^R/k^P must decrease (perhaps due to a more realistic negative effect of fertility on k).

6. Equalizing the return across rich and poor countries,

$$(1-\tau^{rich})(k^{rich})^{\alpha-1}(g^{rich})^{\mu(1-\alpha)} = (1-\tau^{poor})(k^{poor})^{\alpha-1}(g^{poor})^{\mu(1-\alpha)},$$

allows us to solve for the ratio of capital intensities as

$$\frac{k^{rich}}{k^{poor}} = \left(\frac{1-\tau^{rich}}{1-\tau^{poor}}\right)^{\frac{1}{1-\alpha}} \left(\frac{g^{rich}}{g^{poor}}\right)^{\mu}.$$

If fiscal policies differ across countries, so will private capital intensities. In our calibration, $\tau^{rich} < \tau^{poor}$ and $g^{rich} > g^{poor}$, so $k^{rich} > k^{poor}$.

7. The lifetime budget constraint becomes

$$c_{1t} + \frac{c_{2t+1}}{R_t} + n_{t+1}\eta(1-\tau_t)w_t D_t h_t = $$
$$(1-\tau_t)w_t D_t h_t + n_{t+1}(1-\tau_t)w_t D_t \gamma \bar{h}\left(T-e_t\right) + n_{t+1}v(1-\tau_t)w_t D_t \gamma \bar{h}\left(e_t - \bar{e}\right)$$

Maximizing utility subject to this budget constraint leads to the following first order conditions for schooling and fertility,

A Complete One-Sector Model

$$\frac{\psi\theta}{e_t} = \lambda_1 n_{t+1}(1-\tau_t)w_t D_t \gamma \overline{h}(1-v)$$

$$\frac{\psi}{n_{t+1}} = \lambda_1(1-\tau_t)w_t D_t \left(\eta h_t - \gamma\overline{h}(T-e_t) - v\gamma\overline{h}(e_t-\overline{e})\right).$$

Using the same procedure that is followed in *Problem 1* yields the solution.

8. The lifetime budget constraint becomes

$$c_{1t} + \frac{c_{2t+1}}{R_t} + n_{t+1}\eta(1-\tau_t)w_t D_t h_t =$$
$$(1-\tau_t)w_t D_t h_t + n_{t+1}(1-\tau_t)w_t D_t \gamma\overline{h}(T-e_t) + v$$

The first order conditions for schooling and fertility are the same as in *Problem 1*. This implies that the solution for schooling is unaffected by the lump-sum transfer (the solution procedure to get optimal schooling is identical to that in *Problem 1*). The solution for fertility, however, is impacted by pure income effects. The solution for fertility becomes

$$n_{t+1} = \frac{\psi}{1+\beta+\psi} \frac{1+v/(1-\tau_t)w_t D_t h_t}{\eta - (\gamma\overline{h}/h_t)(T-e_t)}.$$ The transfer raises fertility.

Chapter 6
Two Sector Growth Models

Reader's Guide

Section 6.1   From Stagnation to Growth

Purpose: We now consider an economy with two sectors: a traditional sector (producing with labor, land, and crude tools) and a modern sector (producing with labor, certain natural resources, and sophisticated physical capital). Until section 3, one should interpret the output of each sector as the same good produced in different ways (crops produced with a spade versus crops produced with a plough or tractor or cloth made by hand aided by simple wooden spinning wheels versus cloth made with the cotton gin and the steam powered spinning mule). The main issue is to identify when a modern mode of production, that allows for sustained growth via capital accumulation and refinement, can profitably replace a traditional mode of production with less growth potential.

Sticking Points: (i) The condition determining the appearance of a modern sector is given by (6.7). Satisfying this inequality implies modern production is profitable. More precisely, it means capital can earn a return at least as high as land while paying workers what they can earn in the traditional sector.
(ii) Over history, population growth and the development of more secure property rights created ideas about profitable machine-driven production. Eventually, this led to the appearance of modern production in factories.
(iii) The take-off of modern production varied across the world due to differences in the relative TFP in the traditional and modern sectors ($A / \tilde{A}$), due to differences in abundance and quality of land, and in the protection of property rights and other policies affecting modern production.

Take-away: For a modern sector to appear, the technology associated with using machines and factories must reach a profitable level, a level that can vary by country because of land and policy differences.

Section 6.2   The Structural Transformation of a Two-Sector Economy

Purpose: When the modern sector appears, it does not initially dominate the traditional sector; both sectors operate for an extended period. This section studies the dynamics of the two sector economy.

Two Sector Growth Models 81

Sticking Points: (i) The model now determines the values of three key variables k_t, π_t (the share of the workforce employed in the modern sector), and p_t^L (the price of land).
(ii) The dynamics of the two-sector model is fundamentally more complex than the one sector model of previous chapters. This section focuses only on the steady state, bypassing the dynamics of how the economy gets there.
(iii) Under reasonable assumptions, the traditional sector eventually shuts down and land rents converge to zero. However, (unproductive) land may continue to be held as an asset because a "bubble" of rising land prices is possible.

Takeaway: Traditional and modern sectors can coexist for some time in developing economies. During this transitional growth period two new forces affect capital intensity: a growing fraction of workers in the modern sector (lowering k_t) and a declining value of land (raising k_t).

Section 6.3   Two Sectors and Two Goods

Purpose: Examine a two-sector economy with *different* goods produced in each sector: agricultural and primary goods in the traditional sector, manufacturing and service goods in the modern sector. This model gives a more complete picture of development dynamics and also explores how international trade affects growth.

Sticking Points: (i) The analysis begins in a closed economy, where the relative price of the agricultural good equilibrates demand and supply as in a standard micro-model but now with a growth tie-in. This tie-in plays a role in the interesting result that capital accumulation *does not* alter the share of labor used in agricultural. This result suggests the structural transformation away from agricultural is more likely to be caused by other features (e.g. an open economy, population growth, or technological progress).
(ii) In an open economy, the relative price of agricultural goods is determined externally in world markets. In this case, capital accumulation *does* reduce the labor share in agriculture. You will also encounter an exception to the conventional wisdom that trade benefits all participating countries. If a developing country has a comparative advantage in the traditional sector, international trade will make the average household worse off! (See section 8.2 if you want a more nuanced examination of the effects of trade on development.)
(iii) The dynamic analysis of the two-sector model in 6.3.6 is heavy lifting and should be avoided unless the reader has, or is seeking, some advanced training.

Takeaway: In a developing country, the traditional sector is often predominately agricultural. Capturing this feature changes the dynamics of economic growth and brings into question the benefits of opening the economy to the trade of goods.

Section 6.4   Declining Budget Shares Spent on Food

Purpose: Over the course of development, the share of household budgets devoted to food falls (see stylized fact *G10* from chapter 1). Why?

Sticking Points: (i) The standard way of answering the question is to assume that a strict minimum amount of food is needed for survival—a subsistence constraint. This makes food demand disproportionately high when incomes are low.
          (ii) One can "endogenize" the ad hoc assumption of a strict subsistence level of food consumption by explicitly modeling the health benefits of food. The benefits can take many forms but perhaps the simplest is the causal link from calories to body weight to health. An energy balance equation from health science is used in the model of this section to make these links explicit. When including health effects, the marginal benefit of food consumption is high early in development when body mass is low. In developed countries, the marginal health effects can turn negative if body mass becomes too high.

Takeaway: In early development, people tend to have low body mass and the marginal benefit of food is high due to health effects. As income and body mass rise, the marginal benefit of food consumption falls. This is especially true if the energy expended at work also falls.

Solutions to Exercises

Questions

1.   For most of human history there was virtually no sustained increase in per capita income. Before 1700, per capita income was stagnant across the world. England began to see some sustained increases in per capita income during the 18th century, but the growth rates in per capita income were modest, certainly less than one percent per year. Before 1800, the growth rate in per capita income in Western Europe as a whole was barely above one-half percent. In the U.S., growth rates in per capita income were close to zero before 1800. The lack of significant sustained growth in any particular region meant that living standards did not differ dramatically *across* regions. In 1820, Western Europe had per capita income that was at most 2 or 3 times higher than in poor regions.
     After 1800, the nature of economic growth changed. The modest growth in England accelerated and spread throughout Western Europe. Income per capita grew between 1.5 and 2.5 in Western Europe and in the U.S. Not all countries began modern growth in the 19th century. As a result, the income gaps between countries began to grow—a phenomenon known as the *Great Divergence*. Dramatic gaps formed between the richest and poorest countries of the world. Western offshoots such as the United States, Canada, Australia, and New Zealand, formed the richest set of countries in the world by the middle of the 20th century. The per capita

Two Sector Growth Models

income of these countries in 1950 was 15 times, and in 2000 was 18 times higher than those in Africa.

2. The price of land is what the owner receives from selling a unit of land. The rental rate of land is analogous to the rental rate of physical capital. The rental rate from land is what the owner receives when he rents the land out to be used in production—i.e. the flow of output that is attributed to the use of land in production. The return from owning land is the rental income received plus the price at which the land is sold divided by the price that the owner paid to acquire the land.

3. Let's start with the wage rate given in (6.5a). Higher TFP raises the marginal product of labor and wages. We can write out the price of land, by combining (6.5a) and (6.4a), as, $p^L = \frac{\beta}{1+\beta}(1-\alpha)\tilde{A}\tilde{l}^{\alpha-1}$. An increase in TFP also raises the marginal product of land and the land price. Similarly, the rental rate on land from (6.2b) is $r^L = \alpha \tilde{A}\tilde{l}^{\alpha-1}$. An increase TFP raises the marginal product of land and the rental rate paid to landowners. As seen in (6.5b), the return to owning land is unaffected by TFP because the future price and rental rate increase at the same rate as the current purchase price when TFP increases.

To analyze a change in population size, let's again start with the wage rate given in (6.5a). A higher population lowers land per worker and lowers the wage rate. We can write out the price of land, by combining (6.5a) and (6.4a), as, $p^L = \frac{\beta}{1+\beta}(1-\alpha)\tilde{A}\tilde{l}^{\alpha-1}$. An increase in the population size lowers land per worker and raises the land price. Similarly, the rental rate on land from (2b) is $r^L = \alpha \tilde{A}\tilde{l}^{\alpha-1}$. An increase in the population size lowers land per worker and raises the rental rate paid to landowners. As seen in (6.5b), the return to owning land is unaffected by the higher population because the future price and rental rate increase at the same rate as the current purchase price when the population increases.

4. Start with the equilibrium when there is only a traditional sector. There is a rental rate paid to human capital and a return paid to landowners associated with this equilibrium. The question is whether modern firms can produce profitably while paying labor at least the human capital rental rate paid to traditional workers and paying owners of physical capital at least the return earned by landowners. Using these minimum factor price requirements, the condition for nonnegative economic profit in the modern sector can be used to establish a minimum value for the state of technology that is needed for the modern sector to arise.

5. There are several theories of the early progress in D_t that was needed to establish a profitable modern sector. All the theories argue that technological advances occurred very slowly before 1800. Important determinants of the early progress are believed to be the slow and sporadic growth in population size (more people, more ideas), institutional change that encouraged property rights and innovation, and even genetic transmission of the traits that make humans productive (richer people had bigger families than poorer people).

6. For a given state of technology, the threshold condition for a profitable modern sector may or may not be satisfied. There are certain features of economies that play a role beyond just the available state of technology. The minimum technological threshold will be higher in some situations than in others. The threshold is higher for countries with plentiful and productive land or natural resources ($\tilde{A}\tilde{l}^{\alpha}$), a type of "natural resource curse." For example, Habbakuk (1962) argued that United States labor productivity in traditional agriculture was high in the early 19th century, due to the abundance of productive land, and as a result slowed the structural transformation of the economy. The availability of land and certain natural resources in Africa has often been cited as one reason that its take-off to a sustained modern growth path has been delayed.

Parente and Prescott (2000) stress the importance of political forces that restrict work practices, use of machinery, and adoption of the available technology, all making A low and increasing the threshold for take-off. The most famous historical example of such forces were the Luddites, named after one of their leaders (Ned Ludd), 19th-century English textile artisans who violently protested the machinery introduced during the early stages of the Industrial Revolution. Other guilds, early unions of craftsmen, attempted to block technologies that made their skills less important.

A lack of institutions that support markets, such as property right protection or public infrastructure, lowers TFP in each sector. However, from (6.8), we see that any economy-wide deficiencies that lower A and $\tilde{A}$ proportionally will disproportionately harm the modern sector. This is because a lower value of A lowers the demand for physical capital and profits, for given factor prices. Thus, poor support for markets generally can prevent the onset of modern growth. See *Question 7*.

7. Public infrastructure, such as roads, can raise TFP in both sectors. However, even if TFP rises equally in the two sectors, there will be a greater advantage to the modern sector. This is because, while land is fixed, the physical capital of the modern sector is a man-made good that can change. The higher TFP will increase physical capital formation, as we have seen in the one-sector growth model, creating an additional productivity boost in the modern sector that does not exist in the traditional sector.

8. In (6.12), even if there is no technological progress, a rising population will shrink the fraction of workers in the traditional sector for any *given* value of k. A larger population implies a lower land-labor ratio. This will cause wages to fall in the traditional sector, creating a wage gap that will induce workers to leave the traditional sector. However, the analysis is more complicated when we think about how k is affected by the growing employment in the modern sector. A complete dynamic analysis of the entire economy is needed to answer the question precisely.

9. There are two main differences made evident by the transition equation (6.11). First, the presence of land as an alternative way of saving lowers the amount of household saving used to

purchase physical capital. Second, the capital-labor depends on the fraction of labor employed in in the modern sector and not only on the population growth rate of the aggregate work force.

10. It is possible for the price of an asset to grow even when there is no apparent fundamental reason that it should. This is known as an "asset bubble." It is even possible for an asset that has no fundamental value, i.e. an asset that is not productive, to have a positive price. In our model, land could have a positive equilibrium price in the steady state even if there is no traditional sector where land is used in production. There are configurations of parameters that generate a steady state with a permanent asset bubble, i.e. land is continually appreciating despite it having no fundamental value. Although, for reasonable parameter settings, bubbles are not possible. With reasonable parameters, eventually capital dominates land as an asset and land prices go to zero in the long run. However, it is interesting to note that perfectly competitive models without uncertainty, or special assumptions about speculative behavior, have the potential to generate permanent asset bubbles.

11. As we saw in Chapter 4, it is possible for economies to get stuck in poverty traps where schooling does not increase past some minimum amount provided to young children that are not able to work. Advances in human capital from educating the work force are an important part of modern economic growth. Economies begin modern economic growth because a sufficiently high level of technology in the modern sector has been reached, but this may not be sufficient to allow the economy to escape the poverty trap associated with schooling, especially in situations where the relative productivity of young workers remains high. Thus, independent efforts to alleviate the schooling poverty trap may be needed to accelerate modern growth.

12. As was discussed in *Question* 6, abundant natural resources can delay the onset of modern economic growth by creating high wages in the traditional sector that must be paid by any firm operating in the modern sector. However, as indicated by the steady state condition (27), natural resources will have no lasting drag on the economy, provided the threshold level of technology is surpassed. In the long-run, the steady state capital-labor ratio is independent of the economy's natural resources in the model.

13. The fraction of workers in the traditional sector is positively affected by the relative price of the agricultural good (which raises wages in the traditional sector) and negatively affected by the capital labor ratio (which raises wages in the modern sector). In a closed economy, the relative price of the agricultural good is affected by conditions within the economy including the capital labor ratio. An increase in the capital labor ratio increases income and raises the demand for agricultural goods. It also pulls workers out of the traditional sector and lowers the supply of agricultural goods. Both of these effects result in a higher relative price for agricultural goods. In a closed economy, as the capital labor ratio increases, the negative direct effect and the positive indirect effect, working through the relative price, exactly cancel, leaving the share of labor in the traditional sector unchanged.

In an open economy, the relative price is determined internationally and is not affected by conditions within the economy. There is no impact of capital accumulation on the relative price. This implies that the negative effect of capital accumulation mentioned above is unopposed, causing labor share in the traditional sector to shrink.

14. De-industrialization can mean two things in our model. First, it can refer to a reduction in the labor share in the modern sector as the international price of the traditional good rises. Second, it can refer to a reduction in the capital-labor ratio as the international price of the traditional good rises. The first is the more common meaning, but the second meaning is ultimately more important because it affects factor prices and household welfare.

In our model, an increase in the international relative price for the traditional good unambiguously reduces the share of labor in the modern sector, even in the steady state. However, a higher price leaves the steady state capital labor ratio unaffected. This happens because a higher price increases the price of land, which diverts savings from capital accumulation. However, by lowering the share of labor in the modern sector it also raises the capital labor ratio. These two effects are offsetting in our model and as a result there is no effect on factor prices measured in terms of the modern sector good.

In the steady state, a rise in the relative price of agricultural goods lowers welfare because it reduces consumption of agricultural goods. So, de-industrialization is associated with a rise in the relative price of agriculture that causes lower welfare precisely because it does *not* affect the capital-labor ratio and income in manufacturing units but lowers purchasing power in agricultural units.

15. We have seen in *Question* 14, that opening the economy reduces the steady state welfare for economies that experience a rise in the relative price of traditional goods. Furthermore, our transitional analysis shows that an economy open to trading goods (not capital) *may* very well converge less quickly to the same steady state value for k than a closed economy does. In this case, if an economy starts below the steady state, the value of k increases more slowly in an open economy. Increases in k raise welfare, so for transitional generations, there may be an added reduction in welfare from opening the economy compared to steady state generations.

16. The standard preferences we use in the text predict that the budget share of each good is constant. This prediction is not consistent with a declining share of household budgets spent on food as economies develop. One way to explain this development fact is to include the health benefits of nutrition. When incomes are low, the marginal health benefits of food consumption are high, causing households to spend a large fraction of their incomes on food. As incomes and food consumption rise, body weights increase towards the level that generates optimal health. This causes the marginal benefit of further consumption to fall more steeply than for other goods and the share of the budget spent on food declines. Furthermore, as economies develop, the energy demands of work fall and the need for food declines. This effect causes a further decline in the marginal health benefit of food consumption and a further decline in the budget share spent on food.

17. The health benefits of food consumption and the declining energy requirements of work explain why the consumption of calories stays relatively constant over the course of development. This is often modeled as an exogenous "subsistence" constraint, where people behave as if there is a minimum amount of calories that must be consumed to function and survive. The subsistence constraint creates a required amount of food consumption that must take place independent of income.

For these reasons, an increase in productivity in the agricultural sector causes a disproportionate increase in the supply of food relative to the demand for food. The excess supply of food causes the relative price of food to fall faster than the productivity of labor rises, resulting in a decline in the *market value* of the marginal product of labor in the agricultural sector. This causes employment in the agricultural sector to shrink.

18. *G8*

Technology had to advance over centuries before a modern sector with production based on centrally located factories could operate profitably and attract labor away from traditional production at farms and small shops. A major advantage of modern production is that manmade capital can expand with the population of workers. The Malthusian trap where rising population lowers the land-labor ratio and worker productivity is broken, allowing for sustained increases in living standards.

The appearance of modern growth differed across countries because of differences in the threshold that technology had to surpass to generate profit opportunities for firms (due to differences in supporting government infrastructure and institutions or in natural resources and land availability). Differences in the timing of the modern growth take-off, caused the *Great Divergence* in living standards.

G9

Gradually over time, the modern sector expands and the traditional sector contracts, as the superior pace of technological progress and capital accumulation raises worker productivity and wages in the modern sector, continually pulling labor out of the traditional sector. In addition to these "pull" factors, workers are "pushed" out of the traditional sector by population growth that reduces land per worker and wages.

G10

At low incomes and low food consumption, body weight is low causing health to be compromised. This situation creates a high marginal benefit of the food needed to maintain and increase body weight. As a result, large fractions of the household budget are spent on food. As incomes rise over time, the health benefits of additional food consumption falls, causing budget shares to shift to non-food items. Additionally, a common feature of modern technological progress is a reduction in the energy requirements of work. The reduced energy-requirements serve to lower the demand for calories, providing a force that opposes the increased demand for food from pure consumption benefits. The relatively constant demand for calories further accelerates the decline in the budget share devoted to food.

Problems

1. In the first case, with $p = \$100$, the return on land is $\dfrac{\$10+\$100}{\$100} = 1.10$. In the second case with $p = \$50$, the return on land is $\dfrac{\$10+\$50}{\$50} = 1.20$. The *rates* of return are 10 and 20 percent. A higher return to land raises the threshold. This is why the saving rate out of income, $\dfrac{\beta}{1+\beta}(1-\alpha)$, is inversely related to the threshold level. A low saving rate lowers the demand for land as an asset resulting in a lower value of p. A low saving rate delays the appearance of the modern sector.

2. From the equations describing household behavior we know that $\beta/(1+\beta)$ is the saving rate out of wages. We also know that wages are a fraction $1-\alpha$ of income. So the saving rate out of income is $\beta(1-\alpha)/(1+\beta)$.

3. Calculate the right-hand-side of (6.8) under the numerical assumptions presented in each case. (a) $(0.30+5)^{0.5} = 2.3022$; (b) $2 \times (0.30+5)^{0.5} = 4.6044$; (c) $2^{0.3333}(0.30+5)^{0.5} = 2.9005$; (d) $(0.30+10)^{0.5} = 3.2094$

High values for $\tilde{A}$ and $\tilde{l}$, and low values for β, raise the value of the threshold.

4. For a 1 percent annual growth rate in D, $0.2202t = \ln(200) = 5.2983$ => $t = 24.0614$, so it will take more than 481 years for the modern sector to appear. For a 0.5 percent annual growth rate in D, $0.1049t = 5.2983$ => $t = 50.5081$, so it will take more than 1,010 years for the modern sector to appear.

Two Sector Growth Models

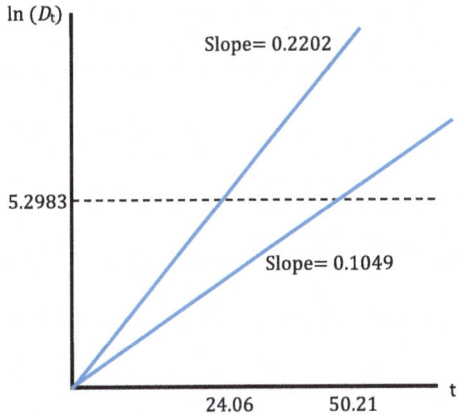

5.   Equation (6.3)   *Household Demand in the Traditional Economy*
Equations (6.3a), (6.3b), and (6.3c) follow as in previous chapters because the household optimization problem is perfectly analogous to those previously encountered except that here households save by buying land instead of physical capital.

    Equation (6.4)   *Price and Return to Land*
The market clearing condition for land requires that the price of land equates the demand for land by households to the supply of available land. Using (6.3c) the land market equilibrium is expressed by $\frac{\beta \tilde{w}_t \tilde{D}_t}{1+\beta} \frac{N_t}{p_t^L} = L$. Solve the land market equilibrium condition for the price of land to get (6.4a). To find (6.4b), start with the definition of the return to land. Then substitute (6.2b) and (6.4a), for periods t and t+1, into the definition. Simplify the resulting expression to get (6.4b).

    Equation (6.8)   *The Threshold*
Begin as indicated in the text, start by writing out the nonnegative condition for economic profits and pull out employment to get $A(K_t/M_t)^\alpha D_t^{1-\alpha} - w_t D_t - r_t(K_t/M_t) \geq 0$. Next, using the first order condition for the profit maximizing physical capital choice, write the capital-labor ratio in terms of the return to capital. Substitute the resulting expression into the nonnegative profit condition and rearrange terms to get $D_t A^{\frac{1}{1-\alpha}} r_t^{\frac{-\alpha}{1-\alpha}} \alpha^{\frac{\alpha}{1-\alpha}} (1-\alpha) - w_t D_t \geq 0$. Finally, use the conditions that the rate of return paid to capital owners must equal that of landowners and the wage paid to modern sector workers must equal that paid to traditional sector workers and substitute into the nonnegative profit expression above to get (6.8).

6.   Plotting $\tilde{w}$ on the vertical axis and N on the horizontal axis produces a downward sloping sketch of (6.5a). An increase in technology would shift the entire curve upward. For a given population size, workers would receive higher wages. Malthus argued that the increased prosperity would result in higher fertility and a larger population. The population would increase until the wage was driven back to whatever it was initially, a subsistence wage that would allow households to just get by. The population size effect would be exhibited as a movement down along the new curve as N increases, until the economy returns to the same wage it had with a lower technology and lower population. Fertility in the new position would once again be low enough to just maintain the new population size.

7.   Equation (6.10)   *Saving in the form of Physical Capital*
This equation is derived by first solving for household saving. Note that because in equilibrium the returns to capital and land must be equal, we can add the two types of saving together and solve for the total saving of the household, which, as usual, takes the form $\dfrac{\beta}{1+\beta} w_t D_t$. Equation (6.10) simply says that saving via physical capital purchases is total saving minus land purchases.

   Equation (6.11)   *The Transition Equation for the Capital-labor Ratio*
Equation (6.11) follows by using the condition that the total capital stock next period must equal the savings devoted to capital purchases this period. Next, use the definition of the effective labor supply in the modern sector to form the capital-labor ratio. Substituting (6.10) for saving via physical capital purchases and using the condition that wages equal the marginal product of labor, completes the derivation.

8.   For simplicity set $D_t = 1$ and then write out the wage equations as
$\tilde{w}_t = (1-\alpha)\tilde{A}(L/(1-\pi_t)N_t)^\alpha$ and $w_t = (1-\alpha)A(K_t/\pi_t N_t)^\alpha$. Sketch each curve as directed in the question. The equilibrium is determined by the intersection of the two curves. Increases in L and $\tilde{A}$ shift the traditional sector wage equation up and reduce π_t. Increases in K and A shift the modern sector wage equation up and increase π_t.

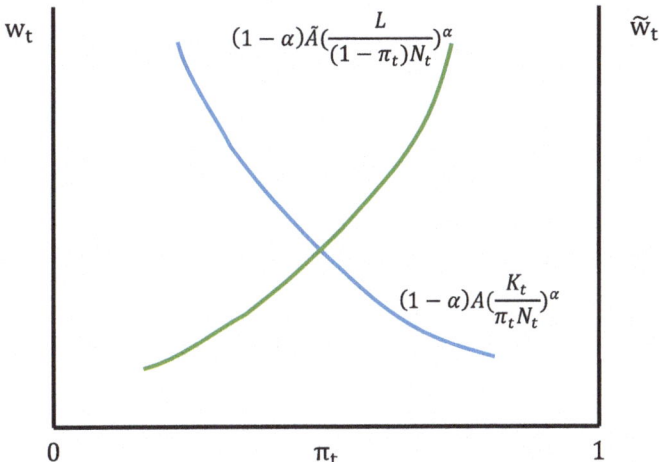

9. Equation (6.19)   *Household Demand with Two Goods*
As in solving for equation (6.10), start the problem by combining the two forms of saving into total saving with the common return R. Next, derive the first order conditions in the usual fashion. As in solving other optimization problems in the book, solve for all other choice variables in terms of the *numeraire in present value*, the good with a relative price of one. Substitute these solutions into the lifetime budget constraint and then solve for the numeraire, which in this case is y_{1t}, to get (6.19a). Use (6.19a) to get solutions to the other choice variables that you previously related to y_{1t}, including total saving which is connected to y_{2t+1} via the second period budget constraint. Finally, derive (6.19d) by subtracting land purchases from total saving.

Equation (6.25)   *The Transition Equation Once Again*
The same procedure used to derive (6.11) can be used here.

Equation (6.28)   *Dynamics using a Linear Approximation*
Take a Taylor linear approximation of functions F and G with respect to the capital labor ratio and land price in period t and t+1, evaluated at the steady state (consult a calculus text for the Taylor approximation, if needed). Use $r = \alpha A k^{\alpha-1}$ and (6.26) to simplify the derivatives of F and G while forming the Taylor approximation. Organize expressions to place the approximation in the form given in (6.28).

10. Using (6.21) the traditional wage equation is

$\tilde{w}_t = (1-\alpha)A(K_t/\pi_t N_t)^\alpha \left(\dfrac{(1-\chi)(1-\alpha)}{1+\beta}\right)^\alpha (1/(1-\pi_t))^\alpha$ and the modern sector wage is

$w_t = (1-\alpha)A(K_t/\pi_t N_t)^\alpha$. To more easily see that a unique equilibrium π_t does exist, plot $\tilde{w}_t/w_t$ against π_t. In equilibrium $\tilde{w}_t/w_t = 1$. Increases in L and $\tilde{A}$ have no effect on the traditional sector wage equation and therefore leave π_t unchanged. Increases in K and A shift both wage equations up proportionally and leave π_t unchanged.

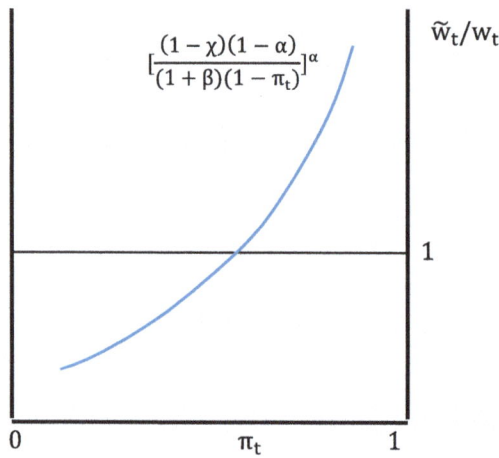

In an open economy we have the following new expression for the traditional wage,

$\tilde{w}_t = p^w(1-\alpha)\tilde{A}l_t^\alpha (1/(1-\pi_t))^\alpha$. Sketching this expression, and the one for w_t, as functions of π_t yields a configuration like that of *Problem 8*. The results of changes in L, $\tilde{A}$, K, and A are the same as in *Problem 8*. An increase in p^w shifts the traditional sector wage curve upward and lowers the equilibrium value of π_t.

11. Combine (6.31a) and (6.31b) to form a quadratic equation that can be used to find values for the two roots. Plug in different combinations of values for β and χ, and then compute the corresponding solutions for the eigenvalues. The finding of two positive eigenvalues with one greater and one less than one is not universal but is quite robust.

For example, suppose households are more impatient than previously assumed so that β is 1/3 instead of ½. If all other parameters are set as in the text, we have $r = 2$ and $\kappa = 1.8$, causing (6.31) to take the form, $\lambda_1 + \lambda_2 = 3.80$ and $\lambda_1\lambda_2 = 1.2$. Combining the two equations gives us $\lambda_1 + \dfrac{1.2}{\lambda_1} = 3.80$. Using either the quadratic formula (see the Technical Appendix) or a little trial and error, the solution is $\lambda_1 = 0.3475, \lambda_2 = 3.4532$, the same "saddle-point" configuration as in the text case that generates a unique equilibrium path to the steady state.

12. Substitute the solutions in (6.19) back into the utility function and write out the terms that are influenced by factor prices and the world relative price. Household welfare is positively affected by factor prices and negatively affected by the world relative price. We established that k is unaffected by changes in the world relative price. This implies that the factor prices are also unaffected. Thus, a higher world relative price makes households unambiguously worse off.

13. Note that $\lambda_1 = \alpha/\pi$ and $\lambda_2 = 1+r$ satisfy the eigenvalue conditions associated with matrix P for the dynamic system in (6.34). For nonnegative interest rates, λ_2 is unstable. A unique and convergent path to the steady state is only possible if $\pi > \alpha$.

14. Equation (6.35) *Budget Shares with a Subsistence Constraint*
Given the adjustments to the preferences associated with food consumption, begin by obtaining the first order conditions in the usual manner. Proceed as before by solving for other variables in terms of y_{1t}. Substitute these expressions into the lifetime budget constraint and solve for y_{1t}. Substitute the solution for y_{1t} back into the expressions for the other variables to get the household demand functions. Finally, write out optimal expenditures on each good and divide by household wages to get the expenditure shares in (6.35).

Equation (6.37) *First Order Conditions with a Health Effect*
Equation (6.37) combines the first order condition for y_{1t}, to eliminate the Lagrange multipler, with the first order condition for o_{1t} and then rearranges to have marginal benefits on the left-hand-side and the marginal cost on the right-hand-side.

Equation (6.38) *Labor Allocation with a Subsistence Constraint*
The supply of output from the traditional sector is $\tilde{A}L^\alpha \left((1-\pi_t)N\right)^{1-\alpha}$. Using (6.20), the supply can be written as $N\tilde{A}\dfrac{l_t}{k_t}(p_t\tilde{a})^{\frac{1}{\alpha}-1}k_t^\alpha$. Demand for the traditional sector good is $N\left[\dfrac{1-\chi}{1+\beta}\dfrac{w_t}{p_t}+\dfrac{\beta+\chi}{1+\beta}\bar{o}\right]$. Equating supply and demand expressions, one can solve for a budget-share based expression for $\dfrac{l_t}{k_t}(p_t\tilde{a})^{1/\alpha}$, yielding (6.38).

15. The dashed curve in Figure 1 gives the marginal benefit of food intake when there are no health benefits ($\kappa = 0$ in equation (6.37)). Along the dashed curve, y_{1t} and o_{1t} increase proportionally with wages as the economy grows, for a constant p. With $\kappa > 0$, the marginal benefit of food exceeds the pleasure of eating when incomes are low, causing food to be a larger fraction of the budget than when $\kappa = 0$ (the second term on the left-hand-side of (6.37) is positive). As income and y_{1t} rise over time, o_{1t} rises less than proportionally along the marginal benefit curve, resulting in a falling fraction of the budget devoted to food. This happens because the health benefits of calorie consumption are also falling, making for a steeper decline in the marginal benefit of further consumption. Eventually, as body mass exceeds the optimal level, the health benefits of further calorie consumption become negative.

Chapter 7
Wage and Fertility Gaps in Dual Economies

Reader's Guide

Section 7.1   Wage and Fertility Gaps

In developing countries, wages are relatively low and fertility is relatively high in the traditional and informal sectors. The gaps in wages and fertility across sectors are large. These facts add additional reasons why the structural transformation can cause higher *average* worker productivity growth in the economy. The facts also raise questions. Why don't workers move quickly to take advantage of the higher wages in the modern sector? Is there a common cause for both gaps? Are there simple explanations for the gaps that do not rely on fundamental differences in how the traditional and modern sectors operate?

Section 7.2   Perfectly Competitive Markets in the Traditional Sector

This section provides some simple explanations for the wage gap. However, the explanations are not likely to be sufficient to fully explain the wage gap and are completely silent as to the fertility gap. The remaining sections of the Chapter seek explanations based on more fundamental differences in how the two sectors operate that explain both gaps.

Section 7.3   Missing Land Markets in the Traditional Sector

Purpose: We explain wage and fertility gaps based on the inheritance of land, family-run farms or businesses, and the associated skills acquired in the traditional sector. The bequest and inheritance of these properties are more likely when legal property rights are absence, causing markets for the properties to be incomplete. The timing of the inheritance causes household saving in the traditional sector to be lower than in the modern sector, an additional sectoral difference that is examined in Chapter 8.

Sticking Points: (i) Inheritance of the "family farm" creates an additional source of income. The wealth from the inheritance compensates for lower wages received in the traditional sector during the working period and raises fertility because greater wealth allows households to afford more children without increasing the opportunity cost of raising children.

(ii) Greater fertility raises the *annual* wage gap per worker because hours worked in the traditional are less than in the modern sector due to time devoted to child care.

(iii) As before, greater adult human capital lowers fertility and increases household labor supply. It also is the reason that the fraction of households in the traditional sector falls over time (greater *effective* labor supplied to work the farm reduces demand for the *raw* number of workers).

Take-Away: Inheritance of family property and intangible capital is a distinguishing characteristic of traditional and informal production, explaining important behavioral differences across sectors that connect the structural transformation to economy-wide economic growth.

Section 7.4   Missing Labor Markets in the Traditional Sector

Purpose: Family farms and informal businesses are disproportionately, and sometimes completely, dependent on family labor. This section shows how the absence of a functioning market for labor affects work effort in the traditional sector.

Sticking Points: (i) The absence of a labor market affects optimal labor supply. When supplying work to a competitive labor market, the worker accepts the wage as a given and decides how much to work. When supplying labor on a family farm, the worker's reward to work is the marginal product of labor. Diminishing marginal productivity lowers the reward to work as more hours are worked, causing workers to work less than when supplying labor to a competitive labor market at a fixed wage. This explains why workers in the traditional sector may choose to work less than in the modern sector where complete labor markets are more prevalent.

(ii) The absence of a labor market also reinforces the connection between school and work effort. Even when a labor-leisure choice is optimally made by the household, greater schooling implies less fertility, more leisure time, and more work.

Take-Away: The absence of labor markets explains why traditional households work less than modern sector households even without compensation by land inheritance.

Section 7.5   Forces that Bind Us

This section discusses why households are reluctant to leave the traditional sector in history and in current developing countries. The advantages of remaining in the traditional sector go beyond inheritance to include informal community services like credit and insurance. Having to be tied to the traditional sector to receive these advantages has the drawback of limiting labor mobility, creating inefficiency related to labor allocation across sectors.

Section 7.6   Asian Growth Miracles

Purpose: In the latter decades of the 20th century, Asian countries such as the Asian Tigers and China have grown remarkably fast. What role did the structural transformation have in generating this growth?

Sticking Points: (i) The theory of this Chapter identifies three ways that the structural transformation affects the growth rate in worker productivity across the economy: reallocating labor from a low to high productivity sector, expanding parental work effort, and reducing the fraction of the workforce comprised of children.

    (ii) Across fast growing Asian countries, the structural transformation accounted for between ½ percentage point and one percentage point of labor productivity growth—roughly 10 to 20 percent of growth.

    (iii) While the African continent has grown faster over the turn of the last century, it lags Asian growth by 3 percentage points. Almost 2/3 of the difference in growth is due to differences in labor flows across sectors. Unlike Asia, Africa has experienced de-industrialization with a flow of labor out of manufacturing and services back to agricultural and primary product production.

Take-Away: The structural transformation has a significant positive effect on aggregate growth. A reverse migration, back to traditional sectors, can undermine a country's development.

Section 7.7 *Productivity Gaps*

There are clearly large gaps in annual wages and worker productivity across sectors of developing countries. The gaps are created by gaps in productivity per hour, hours worked, education, and the return to education of school-aged children, all higher in the modern nonagricultural sector. Movement of households into the modern sector is an important source of average productivity gains for these reasons. Whether the worker productivity gains are closely associated with gains in economic efficiency is more difficult to determine.

Section 7.8 *More on the Misallocation of Labor*

This section reports on evidence suggesting that reducing labor market discrimination and providing more equal access to education for women and minorities was an important source of growth in the later stages of the U.S. economic development.

Solutions to Exercises

Questions

1. There is consistent evidence of large differences in wages and fertility across households that live and work in urban areas and those that live and work in rural areas. In both historical and current day developing countries wages and labor productivity are at least 2 to 3 times higher for nonagricultural workers than for agricultural workers. The fertility gap is also similar in historical and contemporary settings. Rural households tend to have 1.5 more children than urban households.

The gaps in productivity and fertility are connected to economic growth through the internal migration of labor from rural to urban areas associated with the structural transformation. A movement of labor from rural to urban areas will raise average labor productivity and lower the average fertility rate. The increase in labor productivity raises economic growth directly and the reduction in fertility and population growth will raise it through increased physical capital accumulation per worker.

2. *Urban Unemployment*—If one moves to the city, there is a probability of not being employed. Therefore, those that are employed must receive a higher wage than they would get if employed in rural areas. Urban unemployment rates are not large enough to generate large wage gaps, especially when considering that there is rural unemployment as well.

Education Gaps—Urban workers have more education than rural workers and the payoff to education is higher in the urban sector. There is evidence that education also has payoffs in traditional agriculture. In addition, there are large wage gaps even for workers with the same level of education. The relatively low returns to education in the traditional sector may be caused by the more fundamental determinants that cause low parental wages and high fertility leading to low investments in children at early ages.

Unmeasured Home Production—Real wages and productivity are higher than in rural areas than the measured gaps suggest because much of the output in rural areas is unmeasured. This is an important reason for the largest measured gaps in some countries. However, there are detailed household *consumption* surveys that capture untraded production. These surveys reveal large gaps in consumption.

Taxes and Migration Costs—Well-functioning labor markets equate *after-tax* wages. It is easier to tax income in urban areas, so before-tax wages must be higher there, creating a wage gap. In addition, migration costs prevent workers from moving easily across sectors to exploit wages differences. These are reasons for small gaps in wages. Large gaps in wages exist in settings where income taxes are low. The one-time cost of migration would have to be extremely high to prevent workers from exploiting *lifetime* wage gaps.

3. Formal land and labor markets do not exist when (i) the legal institutions do not exist to enforce contractual agreements and property claims and (ii) traditional producers are separated

from each other geographically so that trading is either not possible or infrequent. Wage gaps and the absence of land trading suggest that markets may not exist or do not function well. Historical and contemporary accounts of traditional production give more direct evidence of family-based production where land stays in the family or tribe for generations and where there is little dependence on labor other than family members.

4. The inheritance of the family farm creates residual income for the household. The larger this income is, relative to the opportunity cost of children, the stronger is the demand for children. This is not a pure wealth effect. It is an effect that arises when one form of wealth, residual income from the ownership of family production that does *not* affect the net cost of children, increases relative to another form of wealth, adult earnings from work effort that *does* affect the net cost of children. A shift in the composition of family wealth away from family production and toward adult wages causes the net cost of children to rise, for a given level of total family wealth, and the demand of children falls.

The demand for schooling is not affected by the residual income from family production because of two offsetting effects. To see these effects, first note that fertility raises the cost of schooling children (more children mean greater forgone consumption of parents as schooling rises and child labor income falls). Second, note that the level of parental consumption determines the marginal *value* of forgone consumption associated with greater schooling (higher parental consumption levels means parents can better "afford" the lost consumption associated with more schooling). Family production raises *both* fertility and parental consumption, other things constant. As just mentioned, higher fertility lowers the incentive to educate children, but a higher consumption level raises the incentive to educate children. With our functional forms for preferences and human capital production, these two effects always exactly offset.

5. Under the forgone wage interpretation of the cost of children, the wage gap simplifies to that given by equation (7.11). Equation (7.11) says the wage gap is a constant that exceeds 1, dependent only on the parameters ψ and ρ. This means that items (a)-(c) exert no influence on the wage gap. The gap is clearly increasing in the land share parameter ρ because the greater is the income derived from land relative to wages, the greater is the wage differential across sectors that the traditional household will tolerate before moving to the modern sector. The preference parameter ψ has an ambiguous effect on the wage gap. An increase in ψ causes there to more children and lower total labor supply from a traditional household (due to a reduction in work by parents), which lowers land rents—reducing the tolerance for a wage differential. On the other hand, a higher value for ψ means households place greater value on the larger number of children they have in the traditional sector—increasing the tolerance for a wage differential.

6. Migrants and households remaining in the traditional sector must have the same utility. Due to residual income from the farm, fertility is higher in the traditional sector than it is for migrants. This means that consumption for traditional households must be lower than for migrants, with fewer children, for utility of the two households to be equal. If urban natives have greater schooling and human capital than the migrants, then they will have higher potential

income (and higher utility than both of the other household types). Since consumption is a normal good, this implies that they will also have higher consumption than migrants. Thus, consumption will be highest for urban natives, lowest for traditional households, with consumption of migrant households in the middle.

7. As an economy develops, (a) average fertility falls in both sectors provided schooling rises in both sectors and *average* fertility in the economy falls due to the structural transformation (even with no change in schooling), (b) the wage gap remains constant, (c) child labor falls as schooling rises and *average* child labor in the economy falls due to the structural transformation (even with no change in schooling), and (d) the human capital rental rate in the traditional sector remains constant because the wage gap and the wage in the modern sector are constant.

8. There is evidence that the annual wage gaps in U.S. and European history were predominately caused by differences in hours worked over the year. Wages and productivity on an hourly basis were fairly close between agricultural and nonagricultural sectors, roughly within 25 percent of each other.

There are also hours-gaps in current developing countries. However, they do not explain the majority of the annual wage gaps across sectors. Large, 3 to 4-fold, gaps in wages/productivity *per hour worked* are revealed in the data. At least a significant portion of these hourly gaps are due to gaps in human capital. There is a debate over exactly how much of the hourly gaps is explained by human capital.

9. In cases where there is not only no *national* labor market, but also no *local* labor market in the traditional sector, hours worked will be lower in the traditional sector by choice. The traditional household chooses less work effort than the modern sector household because the diminishing marginal product of labor on the family farm lowers the marginal benefit of work relative to the situation where the marginal reward to work is determined by a perfectly competitive wage rate (that is independent of the household's work choice).

10. As before, fertility is declining in schooling. The main new wrinkle is that now there is a connection between education, fertility, and work. One can show that as e_{t-1} increases, and adult human capital rises, the optimal level of work effort also rises. In most settings with log preferences, the rise in the reward to work has offsetting income and substitution effects that leave work effort unchanged. Here, as human capital rises and fertility falls, time available for leisure increases. The freed leisure time causes a decline in the marginal value of time and lowers the cost of market work. Thus, fewer children mean more time is available for both leisure/home production and market work.

Any difference in schooling across sectors not only increases the productivity gap directly but also does so indirectly by creating a larger gap in market work effort. Just as schooling is one of the fundamental causes of fertility differences across sectors, schooling is also one of the causal factors explaining differences in market hours.

11. Missing markets create advantages to remaining in the traditional sector. Missing land markets make it more likely that land is passed from one generation to the next. The inheritance of land tends to be conditional on the child remaining in the traditional sector to farm the land. Once land is inherited, because secure legal titles over the land do not exist, households must devote significant time to securing the property, making it difficult to participate in the formal labor market. Missing credit and insurance markets cause households to rely on informal provision of these services at the village level, where service providers can monitor behavior effectively.

12. As labor migrates to the modern sector, output per worker will rise directly for three reasons. First, workers are more productive per unit of labor supply in the modern sector (as reflected in the wage gap). Second, households in the modern sector supply more effective labor (since they have fewer children). Third, there are fewer child workers, lowering the supply of labor for a given level of output. This analysis holds constant changes in human capital accumulation and any effects of the structural transformation on saving and physical capital accumulation.

South Korea and Taiwan experienced large reallocations of labor away from agriculture and toward manufacturing during their Growth Miracles. Estimates suggest that the reallocation of labor raised average worker productivity annually by 0.7 percent in South Korea and 0.6 percent in Taiwan.

13. Asia has grown considerably faster than Africa since WWII. McMillan and Rodrik find that the labor flows associated with the structural transformation can explain much of the difference in economic growth between Asian and African countries from 1990 to 2005. While Asian countries have generally experienced a flow of labor away from traditional agriculture and informal urban production, enhancing their economic growth due to the labor productivity gap, African labor flows have gone in the opposite direction, lowering their economic growth. From 1990 to 2005, per capita income in Asian countries grew 3 percentage points higher than in Africa. McMillan and Rodrik estimate that labor flows over this period increased Asian growth by 0.54 percent per year and reduced African growth by 1.3 percent per year. Thus, 1.84 percentage points of the 3-percentage point difference in growth can be attributed to differences in labor flows.

McMillan and Rodrik explain the different experiences of Asian and Africa based on different responses to increased openness of their economies. In labor abundant Asia, international trade created an expansion in the low-skilled manufacturing sector. In resource abundant Africa, openness created an expansion in the commodity and agricultural sectors. In effect opening their economies to trade has caused Africa to "de-industrialize" causing labor to flow from high to low productivity uses.

14. Recent research placed the productivity gap across sectors in the 4 to 6-fold range. Differences in hours worked explain a 1.3-fold gap and differences in years of schooling explain

a 1.4-fold gap for a total gap of 1.82. Explaining the remaining 2 to 3 fold gap is controversial. Some believe it is primarily a measure of inefficiency in the allocation of human capital and others believe it is due to differences in the years and returns to schooling.

15. The indicator of inefficiency in labor allocation is a gap in the marginal product of human capital across sectors. However, the marginal products cannot be observed directly and there is some disagreement about how much they differ across sectors. Even if the marginal products of human capital are similar, the structural transformation can increase average worker productivity by either increasing hours of work or increasing human capital accumulation.

16. Annual wages and annual labor productivity are much lower in agriculture during the early stages of development. A significant portion of the sectoral gap is clearly due to fewer hours worked and fewer years of schooling in the agricultural workforce. The remainder of the gap could be due either to inefficiency in the allocation of human capital or to lower ability and lower quality of education among agricultural workers.

Problems

1. Equation (7.7) *Traditional Household Demand Functions*
The demand for labor given by (7.7c) is found using the condition that the marginal product of labor must equal the traditional sector wage in order to maximize residual income. The equation for schooling in (7.7b) is found in the same manner as in Chapter 4. The same procedure used to derive fertility in Chapter 4, can be used here to get (7.7a).

Equation (7.8) *Wage Gaps*
The indirect utility functions are found by substituting the solutions back into the utility function. The indirect utility function for the migrant is

$\ln\left(\dfrac{w_t \tilde{h}_t}{1+\psi}\right) + \psi \ln\left(\dfrac{\psi}{(1+\psi)(\eta - \gamma(T - \tilde{e}_t)(\bar{e}/\tilde{e}_{t-1})^\theta)}\right) + \psi \ln \tilde{h}_{t+1}$. The indirect utility function for the traditional sector household is

$\ln\left(\dfrac{\tilde{w}_t \tilde{h}_t + (O_t - \tilde{w}_t f_t)}{1+\psi}\right) + \psi \ln\left(\dfrac{\psi\left(1 + \dfrac{O_t - \tilde{w}_t f_t}{\tilde{w}_t \tilde{h}_t}\right)}{(1+\psi)(\eta - \gamma(T - \tilde{e}_t)(\bar{e}/\tilde{e}_{t-1})^\theta)}\right) + \psi \ln \tilde{h}_{t+1}$. Equating the two

indirect utility functions and simplifying gives us $\ln\left(\dfrac{w_t}{\tilde{w}_t}\right) = (1+\psi)\ln\left(1 + \dfrac{O_t - \tilde{w}_t f_t}{\tilde{w}_t \tilde{h}_t}\right)$. Using the first order condition for optimal farm employment, we have $\dfrac{O_t - \tilde{w}_t f_t}{\tilde{w}_t \tilde{h}_t} = \dfrac{\rho f_t}{(1-\rho)\tilde{h}_t}$. Substituting into the expression above and solving for the wage ratio yields (7.8).

Equation (7.11)   Wage Gap Simplified
Substitute the traditional sector labor market equilibrium condition given in the simplified version of (7.9) into (7.8) to get (7.11).

2. The fertility ratio is
$\dfrac{\tilde{n}_{t+1}}{n_{t+1}} = 1 + \dfrac{\rho}{1-\rho}\dfrac{f_t}{\tilde{h}_t} = 1 + \dfrac{\rho}{1-\rho}\dfrac{1-\rho}{1+\psi-\rho} = \dfrac{1+\psi}{1+\psi-\rho}$. If $\rho = 0.40$ and we target $\dfrac{\tilde{n}_{t+1}}{n_{t+1}} = 1.5$, then $\psi = 0.20$. If $\psi = 0.20$, then $\dfrac{w_t}{\tilde{w}_t} = (1.5)^{1.2} = 1.63$.

3. (a) $\dfrac{\tilde{n}_{t+1}}{n_{t+1}} = 1.3846$, (b) $\dfrac{w_t}{\tilde{w}_t} = (1.3846)^{1.2} = 1.4777$, (c) $\dfrac{\frac{1}{1+\psi}}{\frac{1}{1+\frac{\psi}{1-\alpha}}} = \dfrac{0.8333}{0.7692} = 1.08329$,

(d) $1.4777 \times 1.0833 = 1.6008$.

4. The traditional sector household chooses $\tilde{z}_t$ to maximize $\ln \tilde{c}_t + \zeta \ln(v + 1 - \tilde{z}_t)$, subject to the budget constraint, $\tilde{c}_t = l_t^\rho (\tilde{z}_t)^{1-\rho}$. This problem is equivalent to choosing $\tilde{z}_t$ in order to maximize $(1-\alpha)\ln \tilde{z}_t + \zeta \ln(v + 1 - \tilde{z}_t)$. The first order condition for $\tilde{z}_t$ from this problem can be used to solve for $\tilde{z}_t = (1-\rho)\big/\left(1 - \dfrac{\rho}{1+\upsilon}\right) < 1$.

5. The form of the solutions given in (7.13) for the traditional households are the same as those given in (7.12) for the modern households, except that $\tilde{\psi} > \psi$ and $\tilde{\zeta} > \zeta$. The presence of diminishing marginal productivity to family labor $(1-\rho < 1)$ has an effect on behavior that is equivalent to raising the relative value of fertility and leisure time. One can show that this implies $\tilde{z}_t < z_t$ and $\tilde{n}_{t+1} > n_{t+1}$, so traditional households work less and have more children than modern sector households. This is true even if there is no difference in schooling across sectors.

To show that $\tilde{z}_t < z_t$, focus on the denominator of (7.13c). The last expression, contained in the parenthesis, is the same as in (7.12c) because the term $1-\rho$ will cancel out. Any difference in work time is driven by the expression that forms the coefficient of the term in the parenthesis. We want to show that this expression is increasing in $\tilde{\psi}$, which will imply that when $0 < \rho < 1$ and $\tilde{\psi} > \psi$, the coefficient expression is larger in (7.13c). Differentiate the coefficient expression with respect to $\tilde{\psi}$ and show that the sign of the derivative is determined by the sign of $1 - \frac{\gamma T \bar{h}}{\eta h_t}$, which must be positive for fertility to be positive.

For fertility, simply rewrite (7.13b) as

$$\tilde{n}_{t+1} = \frac{\psi(1-\theta)(1+v)}{\eta(1-\rho+\psi+\zeta)} \frac{1}{1 - \frac{\gamma T \bar{h}}{\eta h_t}} > \frac{\psi(1-\theta)(1+v)}{\eta(1+\psi+\zeta)} \frac{1}{1 - \frac{\gamma T \bar{h}}{\eta h_t}} = n_{t+1}.$$

6. We need to show that the denominator of (7.12c) is decreasing in adult human capital. Begin by rewriting the denominator as $1 + \frac{\psi(1-\theta)+\zeta(1-x_t)}{1+\theta\psi-(1+\psi)x_t}$, where $x_t \equiv \frac{\gamma T}{\eta}\frac{\bar{h}}{h_t}$.

Differentiating the denominator with respect to x_t,

yields $\frac{-\zeta[1+\theta\psi-(1+\psi)x_t]+(1+\psi)[\psi(1-\theta)+\zeta(1-x_t)]}{[1+\theta\psi-(1+\psi)x_t]^2} = \frac{\psi(1-\theta)(1+\psi+\zeta)}{[1+\theta\psi-(1+\psi)x_t]^2} > 0$. A higher value of x_t raises the denominator and lowers z_t. So, an increase in schooling lowers x_t and raises z_t.

7. Output can be related to wages using the first order conditions for the optimal choice of employment in the two sectors; $(1-\alpha)Y_t = w_t H_t$ and $(1-\alpha)\tilde{N}_t O_t = \tilde{N}_t \tilde{w}_t f_t$. Solving these equations for output and substituting them into the first equation of section 7.6, the definition of output per worker, gives the second equation of the section. Next, relate the effective labor supplies in the two sectors to human capital and work hours by writing,

$H_t = N_t^*\left(h_t(1-\eta n_{t+1}) + n_{t+1}\gamma\bar{h}(T-e_t)\right)$ and $F_t = \tilde{N}_t f_t = \tilde{N}_t\left(h_t(1-\eta\tilde{n}_{t+1}) + \tilde{n}_{t+1}\gamma\bar{h}(T-e_t)\right)$.

Using (7.4a) and (7.7a), note that $h_t(1-\eta n_{t+1}) + n_{t+1}\gamma\bar{h}(T-e_t) = h_t\frac{1}{1+\psi}$ and

$h_t(1-\eta\tilde{n}_{t+1}) + \tilde{n}_{t+1}\gamma\bar{h}(T-e_t) = h_t\left(\frac{1}{1+\psi} - \frac{\psi}{1+\psi}\frac{\alpha}{1-\alpha}\frac{f_t}{h_t}\right) = h_t\left(\frac{1-\alpha}{1-\alpha+\psi}\right)$. Substituting these expressions into the second equation of the section, rewriting, and using the definition of π_t completes the derivation.

8. From *Problem* 3 and the assumptions made in this problem, we have $\frac{\tilde{n}_{t+1}}{n_{t+1}} = 1.3846$,

$\frac{w_t}{\tilde{w}_t} = 1.4777$, $T - e_t = 0.40$, and $n_{t+1} = 2$. If $\pi_t = 0$, the worker productivity expression in

(7.14) is $\dfrac{w_t h_t}{1-\alpha}\left\{\dfrac{\frac{1}{1.4777}\times\frac{1}{1.3000}}{1+0.4\times 2\times 1.3846}\right\} = \dfrac{w_t h_t}{1-\alpha}\times 0.2470$. For $\pi_t = 1$, we have

$\dfrac{w_t h_t}{1-\alpha}\left\{\dfrac{\frac{1}{1.2}}{1+0.4\times 2}\right\} = \dfrac{w_t h_t}{1-\alpha}\times 0.4630$. The ratio is 1.8743. The structural transformation alone raises worker productivity almost 2-fold.

9. Assume that fertility choices are made first and then, later in the period, schooling decisions are made. Suppose there is an unexpected source of income, z_t, that causes the household to reconsider consumption and schooling choices for a *given* size family. The household maximizes $\ln c_t + \psi\theta \ln e_t$ subject to $c_t + e_t n_{t+1} w_t D_t \gamma \bar{h} = I_t \equiv w_t D_t\left[1 - n_{t+1}\left(\eta - \gamma T \dfrac{\bar{h}}{h_t}\right)\right] + z_t$. The first order conditions are $1/c_t = \lambda_t$ and $\psi\theta / e_t = \lambda_t / n_{t+1} w_t D_t \gamma \bar{h}$. The solutions are $c_t = \dfrac{I_t}{1+\psi\theta}$ and $e_t = \dfrac{\psi\theta}{1+\psi\theta}\dfrac{I_t}{n_{t+1} w_t D_t \gamma \bar{h}}$. An exogenous rise in income raises consumption *and* schooling.

Chapter 8
Physical Capital in Dual Economies

Reader's Guide

Section 8.1 Farmer-Owned Land I—Wage Gaps in US History

Purpose: This Chapter extends the analysis of dual economies to include effects on saving and physical capital accumulation. This section focuses on a dual economy applied to the U.S. in the 19th century.

Sticking Points: (i) Supported by the historical evidence, a constraint on annual hours worked in the traditional sector ($z<1$) is an important feature of the model. The inheritance of land and the benefit of more leisure time compensates young traditional sector workers for accepting less annual income than they would prefer.

(ii) Preferences explicitly acknowledge the value of leaving a bequest via the expression, $\xi\ln(\kappa+\varphi_{t+1}nb_{t+2})$, where ξ and κ are positive preference parameters, φ_{t+1} is the fraction of children that remain in the traditional sector, and b_{t+2} is the bequest per child at the end of period t+1 (when parents die) and received by children in period t+2 (in the second period of their adult life).

(iii) The value of leisure is also represented explicitly by the expression $\varsigma\ln(\nu+1-z)$, where ς and ν are positive parameters. Both new aspects of preferences are included in the utility functions of traditional and modern sector households, i.e. utility functions are the same for all households.

(iv) Saving in the traditional sector is lower than in the modern sector because land ownership provides retirement income and because income when young is lower due to the hours constraint.

(v) Households migrate out of the traditional sector to live in the modern sector. The equilibrium allocation of labor across sectors creates the amount of land inherited per traditional household that exactly compensates for the restriction of work time.

(vi) While the structural transformation increases saving and total capital accumulation it may not increase the capital-labor ratio because the modern sector is absorbing more workers.

Take-away: 19th century U.S. growth in output per worker was raised by an increase in hours worked per *worker* as households moved to the modern sector. There was not much growth in output per *hour worked* because capital intensity in the modern sector was little affected by the structural transformation.

Section 8.2   Farmer-Owned Land II—De-industrialization in the Ottoman Empire

Purpose: Quantify how the large 19th century increase in the relative price of primary products affected de-industrialization, growth, and welfare in the Ottoman Empire.

Sticking Points: (i) The model is a dynamic version of the famous Specific Factors model of international trade. There are three household types: farmers using land to make primary products, craftsmen using physical capital to make manufacturing goods, and migrant laborers who work in either sector.
   (ii) An important result is that technological progress affects the manufacturing and agricultural/primary product sectors differently. In agriculture, technological progress reduces the need for as many laborers to work the fixed amount of land, but total output remains the same. In manufacturing, technological progress does not necessarily reduce the demand for labor if manmade physical capital intensity is maintained or increased, resulting in greater output.
   (iii) A higher international price of primary products causes de-industrialization and slower growth in two ways. First, it increases the demand for farm hands and wages, causing migration out of the manufacturing sector. This slows growth because the economy benefits less from technological change. Second, higher rents from land reduce saving and capital accumulation, lowering wages and further reducing the size of the manufacturing sector.
   (iv) The explicit micro-foundations allow welfare effects for each of the three household types to be computed. While a higher relative price of primary products does cause de-industrialization and slower economic growth, the welfare effects are more nuanced.

Take-away: International trade in the 19th century greatly increased the relative price of primary products in the Ottoman Empire. Despite the resulting de-industrialization and slower growth, the welfare of most households rose. Farmers and migrant workers were both better-off, with the cost of slower growth borne only by craftsmen.

Section 8.3   Other Theories of Trade and Growth

Purpose: Summarize other mechanisms through which international trade may undermine economic growth in developing economies.

Sticking Point: The theories in this section are quite different but all propose a negative connection between international trade and the economic growth of developing countries that have a comparative advantage in primary products. Sections 8.2 and 8.3 offer a surprising contrast to the conventional wisdom that all countries involved in trade are necessarily better off.

Take-aways: (i) Advanced models of production treat skilled and unskilled labor are distinct complimentary inputs. If skilled labor is more important in manufacturing, anything that undermines the expansion of the manufacturing sector reduces the incentive to become educated. An opposing view notes that more educated farmers are more profitable, which poses a challenge to the notion that skilled labor is only valuable in manufacturing.

(ii) Some argue that the proximity of people in urban areas causes ideas to flow more effectively, leading to greater innovation and technological progress. However, the evidence supporting this claim remains mixed. See more on this topic in Chapter 10.

(iii) Up to this point, we have imagined landowners to be small farmers working on their own modest plots. In some countries, landowners are not small farmers but rather wealthy and politically powerful players. It is in the interest of large landowners to keep labor costs low by discouraging policies that raise worker productivity off the farm. This possibility is modeled explicitly in section 8.4.

(iv) There is some empirical evidence that economic uncertainty is correlated with lower average growth rates. In addition, evidence suggests that international trade introduces volatility in relative prices and output, thereby reducing average growth.

8.4 Large Landowners—Growth and Endogenous Fiscal Policy

Purpose: This section shows how the influence of landowners keeps the modern sector, physical capital, and the economy's tax base small, all of which can limit economic growth.

Sticking Points: This entire Chapter, and some of the previous chapters, use *indirect utility functions* to compute welfare and define equilibria. These functions are not assumed directly but rather are derived from the assumed structure of the model. They are the *maximum* utility possible, given the economic environment, formed by substituting the household demand functions back into household preferences. In this section the assumed utility function (*common* to all agents) is given by (8.26) and the three *different* indirect utility functions for each of the three household types (workers, landowners, and government officials) are given in (8.29). The indirect utility functions differ because the household types are affected differently by fiscal policy.

Take-Aways: There are two main results. First, an increase in the influence of landowners raises tax rates, increases the labor share of the traditional sector, and lowers the economy's physical capital stock and tax base. Second, an exogenous increase in the modern sector labor share (say due to technological progress) causes both the tax rate and the tax base to increase, resulting in more government revenue that could be used for public investment.

Solutions to Exercises

Questions

1. All households have the same preferences. The key differences between landed and landless households relate to constraints. First, due to the absence of a land market, if households do not live in the traditional sector they cannot own land. Second, households in the traditional sector are constrained in terms of the hours they can work throughout the year. Later in the chapter, we also consider the fact that taxes are harder to collect in the traditional sector than in the modern sector. The difference in constraints creates a difference in saving behavior. Saving per household is lower in the traditional sector for two reasons: wages are lower, because of the shorter paid work-year, and there is a smaller fraction of wages that is saved because of the second period income associated with land ownership.

2. The overall effect of the structural transformation on physical capital intensity is ambiguous. There is a positive effect because, as households migrate, the average saving rate rises. However, there is a negative crowding effect associated with migration to the modern sector because of the need to provide more capital to a growing modern sector work force.

   Qualitatively, the transition equation, and the economic forces at work, is like the transition equation from Chapter 6, where we assumed perfectly competitive land markets and unconstrained work effort. There, the relative size of land holdings, as an alternative mode of saving, and the fraction of the workforce in the modern sector both served to slow the growth in capital intensity.

   The main difference for capital accumulation is that without a land market, the traditional households that inherit land are the ones who save less in the form of physical capital (and may even borrow). With land markets, the saving of *all* households are equally diverted away from physical capital when land is purchased. The relatively low saving of traditional sector households creates a positive effect on capital accumulation associated with the structural transformation that was not present when there were perfectly competitive land markets in Chapter 6. Now, the saving rate of the economy will rise as households move from the traditional to the modern sector because of the different saving behavior of the households in the two sectors.

3. Labor productivity per hour worked is simply k_t^α, while labor productivity per worker is $k_t^\alpha \left[\pi_t + (1-\pi_t)\tilde{z} \right]$. The structural transformation can only affect labor productivity per hour indirectly by altering the economy's capital intensity. However, the structural transformation has a direct effect on labor productivity per worker because as labor moves from the traditional to the

modern sector, hours worked increase. This distinction can be quite important, as in the case of U.S. economic growth in the 19th century.

During the 19th century, there were large differences in the two growth rates. The annualized growth rate for output per worker was 1.36 percent over the 19th century compared to 0.65 percent for output per hour worked. An average growth rate in output per worker that was double that of output per hour worked supports the claim that the main cause for lower output per worker in agriculture was fewer hours worked. As farm workers migrated to industry over the century, output per worker expanded significantly due to an increase in hours worked per worker. Output per hour worked did not increase as much because farm workers' hourly productivity was not much different from that of nonfarm labor. This means the conflicting effects of the structural transformation on k must have approximately offset.

4.   There are three types in the model: migrants, craftsmen, and farmers. The three types are intended to broadly capture three important groups in the Ottoman Empire during the 19th century. There were migrant workers without land, special skills, or monopoly rights to operate a shop in the city. They sought work in the country and the city. Craftsmen were either skilled workers or government supported entrepreneurs that ran small shops in the city. Farmers were those that had some claim to land that they worked and managed in the countryside.

5.   Craftsmen receive rental income because they have some monopoly power derived either from special skills they possess or because the government has granted them a license to operate a shop in the city (that could be operated by anyone equally well). The rental income or skill premium received by the craftsman is increasing in (i) the output share associated with their contribution to production ($1-\alpha-\bar{\alpha}$) and in (ii) the number of migrants workers used in production (m_I), which raises the craftsman's marginal productivity and lowers the unskilled worker's marginal productivity. Sufficiently high values for the craftsmen's output share or the migrants employed in manufacturing, cause the skill premium to exceed one (see (8.17c)).

6.   De-industrialization can mean a lower share of the workforce and/or a lower capital-labor ratio in the modern manufacturing sector. International trade lowers the modern sector's labor share if the country has a comparative advantage in the agricultural sector (i.e. the international relative price of agricultural goods is higher than the relative price in the closed economy). A higher relative price of the agricultural good also raises land rents and reduces the need to save, thereby reducing the capital-labor ratio. Thus, the direct effects of international trade cause de-industrialization under both meanings.

The analysis of the Ottoman economy reveals that international trade dramatically slowed the migration of workers to urban areas. The effect on capital intensity was much less dramatic. As mentioned, a rise in p lowers $\hat{k}$, other things constant. However, wages in manufacturing were driven up by opening the economy and this causes $\hat{k}$ to increase. Overall, interest rates were a bit lower and $\hat{k}$ a bit higher in the open economy.

7. (a) From (8.21) we see that population growth will increase the supply of unskilled workers and drive the unskilled wage rate down. However, an increase in the relative price of the traditional good raises the demand for labor and drives the wage up. During the two periods over which the relative price rose, the latter effect dominated, and wages rose. After the relative price stabilized, the supply side effect dominated, and wages fell. We will note in (b) that the de-trended capital stock rose over the century. This helped boost the demand for labor and kept wages from falling as fast as they otherwise would have. (b) The urban share and the employment of unskilled labor in the manufacturing sector modestly increased over the century. From (17a), this raises the return to capital and the interest rate. Thus, for the interest rate to fall, the de-trended capital stock must have risen. (c) The skill premium expression in (8.17c) tells us that the skill premium is proportional to unskilled employment in manufacturing. The rise in urbanization indicates that the skill premium should have trended upward over the century. However, this trend was temporarily interrupted when the relative price of traditional goods rose and urbanization was reversed. (d) The land rent of an individual farmer falls because population growth dilutes land ownership. However, this trend was broken when the relative price of traditional goods rose enough to push land rents higher for two periods.

8. By comparing the historical simulation with the counterfactual (constant relative price) simulation we can get a sense of how opening the economy, and the associated jump in the international price, affected the Ottoman economy in the 19th century. In the historical simulation the growth rate in per capita income was 0.78 percent per year. If the relative price is kept counterfactually constant, the growth rate rises modestly to 0.91 percent. So, opening, the economy has a weak negative effect on per capita income growth.

Welfare effects are more complex because they can differ across the three types and across the generations of each type. Table 6 summarizes the welfare effects of preventing the rise in the relative price. Not surprisingly, all generations of craftsmen are made better-off, and all generations of farmers worse-off, when eliminating the relative price increase. For migrant workers it depends on the generation.

For the initial generation of migrants eliminating the price-rise makes them better off. The price increase did not begin until 1840 and so did not affect the wages of the young workers in 1820. However, the higher price of food lowers purchasing for these households when they are old and lowers their lifetime welfare. Eliminating this price rise raises their welfare. Starting in 1840, eliminating the rise in prices also affects wages. Wages would have been lower if the strong demand for labor by the agricultural sector was eliminated. The main result from Table 6 is that, starting in 1840, migrant workers would have been worse off had the international price of food not risen and pushed wages higher.

9. We presented four complimentary theories of how opening the economy of a developing country may lower its economic growth. First, assuming that skilled labor is more important in the modern sector, higher relative prices in the traditional sector may lower the demand for skilled labor and reduce human capital accumulation. Second, it is often assumed that there is a productivity advantage of producing manufacturing goods in urban locations rather than

producing primary commodities in rural locations. Third, landowners will tend to oppose policies that promote physical and human capital formation that impact worker productivity more in manufacturing than in traditional agriculture. The greater is the relative size of the urban population, the more interest there is in promoting capital formation and the more likely the interest of the large landowners can be defeated, setting the stage for more pro-growth policies. Finally, studies consistently show greater volatility is associated with lower average growth rates Opening the economy can increase terms-of-trade volatility and output volatility.

10. This is a difficult question that requires much more research before a clear answer can be given. We know that physical capital inflows can greatly benefit a low saving, developing economy. Capital inflows not only speed transitional growth but can have long-run steady state impacts as well if fiscal policy becomes more pro-growth. The effects of trading goods are more complex.

Our model suggests that trade can slow down or even reverse the structural transformation. There are several complimentary theories that associate a weaker pace of structural transformation with a weaker pace of economic growth. However, we have also seen that if the negative growth rate effects from opening the economy are not large, then most generations of most household types could nevertheless benefit from trade. There currently is no short or bottom-line answer to this important question.

11. Consult the indirect utility functions given in (8.29). A higher tax rate lowers the after wage of workers and makes them worse off. A higher tax rate raises the welfare of landowners. Workers avoid the tax by reallocating work effort to the traditional sector. This drives down the traditional wage, increases farm employment, and raises the land rents of landowners. Finally, government officials benefit from a higher tax rate, provided that the exit from the taxable modern sector is not too great.

12. If landowners have more power and receive a greater weight in determining policy, the tax rate will increase because they like the fact that it will cause workers to exit the modern sector, increasing the supply of labor and lowering the wage in the traditional sector. The exit of workers from the modern sector causes the economy's total capital stock to fall.

13. The first explanation is based on exogenous factors that cause the size of the modern sector to grow. An increase in π_t for a given tax rate, lowers the marginal cost of taxation and causes the optimal tax rate to increase. The intuition is that the *marginal* loss in the tax base as the tax rate rises is less valuable the larger is the *total* tax base. Thus, tax rates will tend to increase, other things constant, as economies grow and modernize.

The second explanation for the growth in the size of government is related to the growth in social transfers. This reason for the growth in government tends to occur in later stages of development as countries become more democratic.

14. For *Question 12*, an increase in $\tilde{\phi}$ lowers the marginal cost of taxation (landowners like the fact it increases the supply of labor in the untaxed traditional sector and lowers wages there), shifting the marginal cost curve in Figure 1 downward and increasing the optimal tax rate. For the first explanation in *Question 13*, an increase in π_t also lowers the marginal cost of taxation (with a larger tax base, the marginal loss in tax revenue from raising the tax rate is less valued), shifting the marginal cost curve in Figure 1 downward and increasing the optimal tax rate.

15. An increase in ϕ^g increases the marginal benefit of taxation that stems from the marginal utility of consumption by government officials whose salaries are financed by the tax revenue. However, an increase in ϕ^g also increases the marginal cost of taxation because a higher tax rate shrinks the taxable wage bill in the modern sector as workers move to the traditional sector to avoid taxation. If the country is on the upward-sloping portion of the Laffer curve, i.e. if an increase in the tax rate raises revenue, then a marginal increase in ϕ^g will raise the tax rate. This condition is not guaranteed. If the weight on private households is low and the weight on landowners is high, then the tax rate might be so high that a marginal increase in the tax rate lowers revenue. In this case a marginal increase in ϕ^g will lower tax rates because it yields greater tax revenue.

16. The new twist that pertains to *G9* is that households in the two sectors save at different rates. As traditional households give up land claims and move to the modern sector, their saving rate rises. The structural transformation then causes capital to accumulate more rapidly. The accumulation of capital widens the wage gap, everything else constant, a feedback effect that speeds the migration out of the traditional sector.

Government growth is dependent on an expanding tax base. The structural transformation expands the tax base because modern production is easier to tax than traditional production. The model also predicts that an expanding tax base increases the optimal rate of taxation, further increasing the growth in tax revenue and the relative size of government, as stated in *G12*.

The greater the weight placed on government consumption (ϕ^g), the more emphasis there will be on maximizing tax revenue. A high value for ϕ^g can result when one ethnic group gains control of the government within an ethnically fractious country with a weak democracy. This characterizes several developing countries today, helping to explain why their government share is large at an early stage of development.

Problems

1. The landed households maximize the same preferences as landless ones, given by (8.4). Landed households choose consumption and farm labor to maximize (8.4) subject to (8.3) and (8.7). The first order condition for farm labor, $(1-\rho)l_{t+1}^{\rho}f_{t+1}^{-\rho} = w_{t+1}$, can be used to write $O_{t+1} - w_{t+1}f_{t+1} = \rho O_{t+1}$. Solving for first period consumption in the usual way, gives us

$$\tilde{c}_{1t} = \frac{w_t \tilde{z} + \frac{\rho O_{t+1}}{R_t}}{1+\beta}.$$

Substituting into the first period budget constraint, $\tilde{c}_{1t} + s_t = w_t \tilde{z}$, and solving for saving, yields (8.8a).

2. The indirect utility functions for landless and landed households are

$$V_t = \ln\left(\frac{1}{1+\beta}\right) + \beta \ln\left(\frac{\beta}{1+\beta}\right) + \beta \ln R_t + (1+\beta)\ln w_t + \xi \ln \kappa + \zeta \ln v, \text{ and}$$

$$\tilde{V}_t = \ln\left(\frac{1}{1+\beta}\right) + \beta \ln\left(\frac{\beta}{1+\beta}\right) + \beta \ln R_t + (1+\beta)\ln w_t + (1+\beta)\ln \tilde{z} + (1+\beta)\ln(1+\frac{\alpha O_{t+1}}{R_t w_t \tilde{z}})$$
$$+ \xi \ln(\kappa + l_{t+1}) + \zeta \ln(v + 1 - \tilde{z}).$$

Equating the two indirect utility functions, collecting terms, and remembering that $\upsilon = \frac{\zeta}{1+\beta}$, yields (8.9).

To show that Ω_{t+1} is decreasing in $\tilde{z}$, take the natural log of both sides of the expression for Ω_{t+1} and differentiate with respect to $\tilde{z}$. Use $\tilde{z} < 1$ to show that Ω_{t+1} is inversely related to $\tilde{z}$.

3. Using the first order condition for rent-maximizing employment of farm labor, we can write

$$\frac{\alpha O_{t+1}}{R_t w_t \tilde{z}} = \frac{\alpha w_{t+1} f_{t+1}}{(1-\alpha)\alpha k_{t+1}^{\alpha-1}(1-\alpha)k_t^{\alpha} \tilde{z}} = \frac{k_{t+1}}{(1-\alpha)k_t^{\alpha} \tilde{z}}\left[\frac{1}{k_{t+1}^{\alpha}}\right]^{\frac{1}{\alpha}} l_{t+1} = \frac{1}{(1-\alpha)k_t^{\alpha} \tilde{z}} \frac{L}{(1-\pi_t)N_t}.$$ The last equality results from the fact that land per farm is land per old member of the traditional sector, which is equal to the number of young households in the traditional section in period t.

4. Divide (8.12) by $M_{t+1} = \pi_{t+1}N_{t+1} + (1-\pi_{t+1})N_{t+1}\tilde{z} - f_{t+1}(1-\pi_t)N_t$ to get

$$k_{t+1} = \frac{\pi_t s_t + (1-\pi_t)\tilde{s}_t}{n(\pi_{t+1} + (1-\pi_{t+1})\tilde{z}) - f_{t+1}(1-\pi_t)}.$$

Next, using (8.8b), note that labor demand from the traditional sector can be written as $f_{t+1}(1-\pi_t) = \frac{l_{t+1}}{k_{t+1}}(1-\pi_t) = \frac{L}{N_t k_{t+1}}$. Substituting the labor demand expression back into the capital-labor ratio equation and solving for k_{t+1} gives us

$$k_{t+1} = \frac{\pi_t s_t + (1-\pi_t)\tilde{s}_t + \frac{L}{N_t}}{n(\pi_{t+1} + (1-\pi_{t+1})\tilde{z})}.$$ Finally, substitute the household saving functions in the equation to get (8.13).

To simulate the model, we need to determine the fraction of the working population that is allocated to each sector. *Problem 3* establishes that the equation needed to determine this allocation is (8.9). The left-hand-side of (8.9) can be written as a function of $(1-\pi_t)$ and k_t. So, given k_t we can solve for $(1-\pi_t)$. Then we can solve (8.9) and (8.13), dated one period ahead, for $(1-\pi_{t+1})$ and k_{t+1}.

5. The number of young households of our three types are denoted as $\bar{N}_t$ (migrant workers), N_t^* (craftsmen), and $\tilde{N}_t$ (farmers). Labor market equilibrium requires that the demand for workers by craftsmen and farmers (net of young members of the farm households) must equal the supply of migrant workers looking for work, $N_t^* m_t + \tilde{N}_{t-1} f_t - \tilde{N}_t = \bar{N}_t$. Use the fact that $l_t = L/\tilde{N}_{t-1}$, where L is the total amount of raw land available for farming, (8.17b), and (8.19) to solve for the demand for labor by craftsmen and farmers. Now we can rewrite the labor market equilibrium condition as $N_t^* \left(\frac{\bar{\alpha}}{w_t} \hat{k}_t^\alpha \right)^{\frac{1}{1-\bar{\alpha}}} + \left(\frac{(1-\alpha)p_t}{w_t} \right)^{\frac{1}{\alpha}} \left(\frac{L}{D_t} \right) = \bar{N}_t + \tilde{N}_t$.

6. To write total output as (8.25), first note that (8.16) and (8.17) can be combined to rewrite y_t as $D_t \hat{k}_t^\alpha \left(\frac{\bar{\alpha} \hat{k}_t^\alpha}{w_t} \right)^{\frac{\bar{\alpha}}{1-\bar{\alpha}}}$. Next, use the period t version of (8.19) to solve for $D_t f_t$ and then substitute into (8.18) to get the desired new expression for $p_t O_t$. The two new expressions for output in the two sectors can be used to write total output as in (8.25). Technological progress reduces the need for workers but does not increase total output in agriculture. If physical capital increases to match technology, maintaining physical capital intensity, technological progress raises output in manufacturing.

7. Using the first order condition for farm employment we know
$$\frac{rent_{t+1}}{w_t D_t R_t} = \frac{\alpha}{1-\alpha} \frac{w_{t+1} D_{t+1} f_{t+1}}{w_t D_t R_t} = \frac{\alpha}{1-\alpha} \frac{(1+d) f_{t+1}}{w_t} \frac{w_{t+1}}{R_t}.$$ Next,
$$\frac{w_{t+1}}{R_t} = \frac{w_{t+1}}{r_{t+1}} = \frac{\bar{\alpha}}{\alpha} \frac{\hat{k}_{t+1}}{m_{t+1}} = \frac{\bar{\alpha}}{\alpha} \frac{\hat{k}_{t+1} N_{t+1}^*}{\left[\tilde{N}_{t+1} + \bar{N}_{t+1} - \tilde{N}_t f_{t+1} \right]},$$ where the third equality follows from (8.17) and the fourth equality follows from (8.20).

8. Let $\bar{V}_t^M$ denote the welfare of a migrant worker when the relative price is kept counterfactually constant. The change in welfare associated with eliminating the price rise is $\bar{V}_t^M - V_t^M = (1+\beta)(\ln \bar{w}_t - \ln w_t) + \beta(\ln \bar{R}_t - \ln R_t) + (1-\chi)(\ln p_t + \ln p_{t+1})$. Consider 1860, where the loss in welfare is the greatest when $1-\chi$ is 0.75. What value must $1-\chi$ take in order to eliminate the loss in welfare? To find out, set the welfare change to zero and then solve for $1-\chi$. Then plug in the information from Tables 4 and 5 to get a value for $1-\chi$ of 0.9226. Any value of $1-\chi$ above this will cause the migrant worker to gain from eliminating the price rise. We can use the values generated in Tables 4 and 5 because, as mentioned in the text, they are independent of the value of $1-\chi$.

9. First note that, in equilibrium, $\omega_t = (1-\tau_t)w*$. Thus, solving the workers utility maximization problem in the usual way and substituting the solution back into the utility function yields (8.29a). Second, again using $\omega_t = (1-\tau_t)w*$, along with (8.27) and (8.28), allows us to write the indirect utility function for landowners as (8.29b). Finally, the government official's lifetime income can be written as $w_t^g = \dfrac{w*N_t}{N_t^g}\tau_t\pi_t$. Solve the government official's consumption problem as for any other agent. Substituting the solution into the government official's utility function, and assuming the population share of the government remains constant over time, yields the indirect utility function given by (8.29c).

10. The theory in the text allows us to write $1-\pi_t = \dfrac{L}{N_t}\left[\dfrac{1-\rho}{(1-\tau_t)w_t}\right]^{\frac{1}{\rho}}$. Take the log of both sides and differentiate with respect to the tax rate and solve for $\dfrac{d\pi_t}{d\tau_t}$ to get the result.

11. Substitute (8.29) into $\phi^g V_t^g + \phi V_t + \tilde{\phi}\tilde{V}_t$ and maximize the resulting expression by choosing the tax rate. Reorganizing the resulting first order condition yields (8.30).

12. With an income tax, it is the after-tax return to capital that is equalized across countries. This means $(1-\tau_t)r_t = (1-\tau_t)\alpha A k_t^{\alpha-1} = r*$. Solving for k_t gives us $k_t = \left[\dfrac{(1-\tau_t)\alpha A}{r*}\right]^{\frac{1}{1-\alpha}}$.

After tax wages can then be written as

$(1-\tau_t)w_t = (1-\tau_t)(1-\alpha)Ak_t^\alpha = (1-\tau_t)^{\frac{1}{1-\alpha}}(1-\alpha)A^{\frac{1}{1-\alpha}}\left(\dfrac{\alpha}{r*}\right)^{\frac{\alpha}{1-\alpha}}$.

Next, we need to write out the tax revenue collected and used to pay the government officials. Tax revenue becomes $\tau_t(w_t \pi_t N_t + r_t K_t) = \tau_t \pi_t N_t(w_t + r_t k_t) = \tau_t \pi_t N_t A k_t^\alpha$
$= \tau_t(1-\tau_t)^{\frac{\alpha}{1-\alpha}} \pi_t N_t A^{\frac{1}{1-\alpha}} \left(\frac{\alpha}{r^*}\right)^{\frac{\alpha}{1-\alpha}}$. Finally, note that the labor share becomes

$$\pi_t = 1 - \frac{L}{N_t}\left[\frac{1-\rho}{(1-\alpha)A^{\frac{1}{\alpha}}\left(\frac{\alpha}{r^*}\right)^{\frac{\alpha}{1-\alpha}}}\right]^{\frac{1}{\rho}} \frac{1}{(1-\tau_t)^{\frac{1}{(1-\alpha)\rho}}}.$$

The form of the indirect utility functions is the same and we can rewrite them as

(29a') $V_t = E + \frac{1+\beta}{1-\alpha}\ln(1-\tau_t)$

(29b') $\tilde{V}_t = \tilde{E} - (1+\beta)\frac{1-\rho}{\rho(1-\alpha)}\ln(1-\tau_t)$

(29c') $V_t^g = E^g + (1+\beta)\left(\ln \tau_t + \frac{\alpha}{1-\alpha}\ln(1-\tau_t) + \ln \pi_t\right)$.

The choice of the tax rate is qualitatively like the wage tax case. The difference is that raising the tax rate now reduces the capital-labor ratio. This implies a larger negative effect of the tax rate on the after-tax wage because it also lowers the before-tax wage. For the same reason, there is a larger negative effect of raising the tax rate on the tax base. Thus, there is a higher cost to taxation for workers and government officials, but a higher benefit of taxation to landowners. The new first order condition determining the tax rate is

$$\frac{\phi^g}{\tau_t} = \frac{1}{(1-\tau_t)(1-\alpha)}\left\{\phi^g\left(\frac{1-\pi_t}{\rho\pi_t} + \alpha\right) + \phi - \frac{1-\rho}{\rho}\tilde{\phi}\right\}.$$

Note that the marginal benefit on the left-hand side is the same as before, but the marginal cost on the right-hand side is higher. This implies that the tax rate will be lower.

Chapter 9
A Complete Dual Economy

Reader's Guide

Section 9.1 The Dual Economy

Purpose: Develop a model that captures all the essential features of a dual economy that were introduced in earlier chapters.

Sticking Points: (i) The most complicated expression at the household level is the present value of second period residual "farm" income per child remaining in the traditional sector, $\frac{O_{t+1} - w_{t+1}\tilde{D}_{t+1}f_{t+1}}{R_t \varphi_t \tilde{n}_t}$, relative to their first period wages, $w_t \tilde{D}_t \tilde{z} \tilde{h}$. This expression is an important driver of what happens in the model. The relative farm income must be sufficient to compensate traditional households for accepting less work than what is preferred in the first period of life. The required amount of farm income that just satisfies this condition is given by $\Omega \equiv \left(\frac{1}{\tilde{z}}\right)^{\frac{1+\beta}{1+\beta+\psi}} - 1$. The equality between actual relative farm income and the required amount determines how many households remain in the traditional sector and how many leave for the modern sector. The number of siblings from generation-t that operate the farm is some fraction, $\varphi_t \leq 1$, of all siblings ($\tilde{n}_t$). Note also that the second period farm income makes saving lower and fertility higher in the traditional sector.

(ii) The transition equation for physical capital intensity in the modern sector has the same general form as the simpler ones from previous chapters—saving out of current wages relative to the future effective work force used in the modern sector. The future effective work force is complex because it accounts for population change (based on fertility in both sectors), human capital accumulation, technological progress, and different work time across sectors. The effective workforce in the modern sector is found by subtracting the labor demanded in the traditional sector from the total effective work force.

Take-away: The structural transformation affects the growth in capital intensity as follows: (1) a rise in saving due to higher saving rates and greater wage income in the modern sector (raising k) and (2) ambiguous changes in the effective work force in the modern sector as fertility and population growth fall but migration to the city rises (ambiguous effect on k).

Section 9.2 Transitional Growth in the Long-Run

Purpose: Conduct a numerical simulation of the dual economy model and then compare to the historical growth patterns.

A Complete Dual Economy

Sticking Points: (i) The first objective of the simulation is to explain worker productivity growth, given by (9.13d). The structural transformation affects worker productivity growth via physical capital intensity and the effective labor supply per worker. In the simulation, the effective labor supply expands because modern households work more than traditional households (more available hours and less childcare).
             (ii) As noted, the effect of the structural transformation on physical capital intensity is complex. It is worthwhile to study the numerical breakdown of the individual forces given in the text just before the full growth simulation is reported.

Take-aways: Here are the key features of the numerical simulation.
             (1) Growth rates in worker productivity rise over the first century, level off, and then decline at the end of the second century—a "wave-pattern" that matches history (see section 9.3).
             (2) Most of the growth in the first century is due to an expansion of work effort, with physical and human capital accumulation taking over in the second century.
             (3) Schooling rises, modestly at first, and fertility falls throughout, initially more due to the movement away from the traditional sector than due to the rise in schooling. These patterns resemble the historical data from the U.S. found in the introduction to Chapter 4.
             (4) Endogenous sources of growth explain a little less than half of the total rise in worker productivity.

Section 9.3   *Great Waves of Growth*

Purpose: To compare the simulation of section 9.2 to actual growth experiences.

Sticking Points: This section identifies several weaknesses of the model that should be addressed in future research.
             (i) Hours worked in the modern sector tend to decline with in later development rather than remain constant as assumed in the model.
             (ii) In some developing countries, wage gaps per hour worked, and not just differences in work time, are important. This can increase the endogenous explanation of growth.
             (iii) The unusually rapid growth of Growth Miracle countries is not fully explained (see section 9.4 for a discussion).
             (iv) Technological progress is an important source of long-run growth and should be modeled as an endogenous variable. This extension could start with including government investment in infrastructure and basic research, as in Chapter 3.

Take-away: Despite some limitations, the model provides a good foundation for thinking about development because it captures the common wave-like pattern of growth over long period of time.

Sections 9.4-9.8   Discussion

Purpose: These sections introduce a variety of topics related to the formal model.

9.4   South Korea is one of the Growth Miracle Asian Tiger countries. Its onset of modern growth began around 1960 with land reforms that secured property rights for individual farmers, the beginning of a grassroots push for education, and an inflow of U.S. aid for public infrastructure investment (a key factor not captured by the simulation of this chapter). The effects of these changes on labor productivity growth were initially muted by a high rate of fertility and population growth. Growth accelerated when the structural transformation, made possible by the earlier changes, began in earnest. High domestic saving rates and private capital inflows fostered capital formation and development of the modern manufacturing sector. An industrial policy established close ties between the largest firms and subsidized government loans. The government also continued its commitment to infrastructure and R&D investment to maintain high growth.

9.5   There are several ways to expand on human capital investments that would help explain more transitional growth in developing countries. In addition to student time, human capital formation is positively influenced by school expenditures on teachers and textbooks and by the previously accumulated human capital of parents, teachers, and the community at large. Health investments in mothers and infants, such as nutritional supplements, also have significant effects on a child's adult productivity.

9.6   On average, developing countries are not catching up or converging to richer countries. The majority of currently developing countries are growing at the same rate or slower than rich countries. Growth Miracles in poorer countries are the exception not the rule.

9.7   Countries not yet experiencing modern growth often have a powerful group that benefits from the traditional economy and opposes policies that would allow the modern sector to expand (a political poverty trap). We provide examples in Chapters 3 and 5 where government officials seek to raise their own consumption and in section 8.4 where large landowners push policies that raise land rents but hurt growth. The presence of valuable natural resources and an ethnically divided society often create this situation.

9.8   When compared to other countries, the U.S. has significant productivity advantages in the agricultural and service sectors but not so much in manufacturing. This sectoral pattern of relative productivity advantages explains why most other countries have failed to fully converge to the U.S. per capita income. A country that transforms away from agriculture

A Complete Dual Economy

into manufacturing will begin to catch up to U.S. productivity levels. However, when the country develops further and transforms from manufacturing into services, the convergence to the U.S. stalls.

Solutions to Exercises

Questions

1. Land inheritance is certainly an important consideration binding young workers to family production but it is not the only consideration. Young workers also inherit specific skills, local knowledge of productive factors, and business relations based on trust and familiarity with the family. In short, children inherit not only land, but an entire family production technology that is passed down from working with their parents. In some cases, land inheritance is the least important of these factors.

2. Non-wage income from operating the family business raises fertility in the traditional sector relative to the modern sector. Traditional schooling is different from the schooling in the modern sector if there are differences in initial conditions or in γ across the two sectors. The family farm provides income during retirement, a substitute for retirement saving when young. Traditional households have lower wage income because of the constraints on their hours worked. Saving from a traditional household will be relatively low because both their earnings and their saving rate are lower than households in the model sector. Thus, the traditional household will tend to have lower wage income and saving, and higher fertility, than households in the modern sector.

3. We assume a national labor market so that the wages paid to a unit of human capital must be equalized across sectors, $\tilde{w}_t \tilde{D}_t = w_t D_t$. All productivity differences are "annual," based on differences in hours worked, and not due to differences in productivity per "hour." A national labor market requires that the total demand for labor from the traditional sector in each period t, must exceed the supply of labor coming from younger members of traditional households in period t. This means that some of the labor hired in the traditional sector will come from the modern sector.

4. For some households to stay in the traditional sector and other households to leave the traditional sector, households must be indifferent about their locational choice. This implies that the *actual* relative income from the family business must achieve a *required* value in order to just compensate traditional households for the hours-constraint on their work time when young. The more severe the hours constraint, the lower is $\tilde{z}$, the greater must be the relative income from inheriting the family business. The degree to which residual income must compensate for the hours constraint is lessened by the desire to have a large family. Staying in the traditional sector to operate the family business also means having more children (higher wages when young raises

the cost of children, while higher residual income when old does not). Given that parents like children, the wealth compensation necessary for accepting less work hours when young is not as great when families are larger.

The required value of the relative income from operating a family business is important for all relationships in the model that involve the behavior and allocation of households across sectors. Income from the family business provides financing for retirement consumption that reduces saving of traditional households. Greater non-labor income and lower labor income implies that fertility is higher in the traditional sector, even if schooling is the same across sectors. The higher fertility of the traditional household reduces their adult equivalent units of labor supply (combining the labor of parents and children) relative to the modern household. This is because the increase in child labor does not fully offset the lost labor time associated with raising the child. Finally, a higher required value of the relative income from the family business implies more traditional sector households must migrate to the modern sector to increase the share of the family business for the children that remain.

5. The extension to a two-sector dual economy creates two new influences on physical capital intensity. First, the structural transformation releases labor from the traditional sector and increases the growth in the modern sector working population. The size of the migration flow depends on how fast the traditional labor supply is growing relative to the traditional sector demand for labor. Faster growth in the traditional sector labor supply lowers capital intensity in the modern sector. For a given supply of labor in the traditional sector, a decline in the traditional sector demand for labor also releases labor that must be absorbed in the modern sector. The migration flow caused by both of these features causes the modern sector capital intensity to fall.

The negative migration effect of the structural transformation on capital intensity is countered by a second effect that serves to increase capital intensity. Traditional sector households save at lower rates than modern sector households. As households migrate to the modern sector the economy's average saving rate increases and capital intensity rises. Overall, the structural transformation then has an ambiguous effect on physical capital intensity.

The rental rate on human capital is the same throughout the economy because of the national labor market. The rental rate is a function of the physical capital intensity in the modern sector. The structural transformation then has an ambiguous effect on the rental rate because it has an ambiguous effect on physical capital intensity.

6. In *Question* 5 we discussed the ambiguous impact that the structural transformation has on physical capital intensity and the rental rate on human capital. This means that if the structural transformation has a significant impact on economic growth, it must be through some other mechanism.

One clear mechanism through which growth may be impacted is labor supply. As workers migrate to the modern sector they avoid the hours-constraint and work more. In addition, we know that fertility falls as household migrate to the modern sector. As discussed in *Question* 4, the fall in fertility further increases the adult-equivalent labor supply coming from the family. Thus, the structural transformation will increase economic growth primarily through an increase in work hours.

7. The simulations capture many of the observed features of growth including the "wave-like" pattern of growth rates, declining shares of the work force in traditional agriculture, relatively trendless interest rates, declining fertility, rising schooling, and falling child labor. The main weakness is that a large fraction of observed growth must be modeled as exogenous technological change. Some of what we attribute to exogenous technological change is due to potentially important omitted variables, discussed earlier in the text, such as goods investment in schooling, investments in health, and government investment in public infrastructure. In addition, ultimately one would want to include a theory of how technological change occurs. Finally, the theory is missing important factors that cause the very high growth rates associated with Growth Miracles.

8. The increase in labor supply was the most important long-run factor causing growth. It is particularly important in the early stages of growth. The increase in labor supply is connected closely to the structural transformation as explained in *Question* 6. Human and physical capital accumulation became the maim drivers of growth in the second century.

9. As discussed in Section 9.5 there are certainly additional human capital investments that could have been included, such as the goods inputs to schooling (books, teacher's time, etc.), that we recorded in Chapter 2 for the historical U.S. One could also include investments in health of children and workers. In addition, there is evidence for community externalities that expand the impact of human capital acquired to the human capital acquired by future generations and thereby strengthens the role of schooling investment in explaining transitional growth. We also ignored the fact that some of the growth that is attributed to exogenous technological change is due to government investment in public infrastructure. Finally, the analysis done by Jones suggests that one can interpret much of technological progress as also being "transitory."

10. Our model explains the rise and fall of growth rates as follows. The diminishing returns associated with capital accumulation are initially more than overcome by the gains in work effort and productivity associated with the structural transformation and by rising investment rates. These features of development cause growth rates to rise initially. However, there are ultimately growth slowdowns as investment rates level off and the structural transformation becomes complete.

The wave-like growth pattern offers a pessimistic forecast for growth in the 21st century. One can become even more pessimistic if there are reasons to believe that technological progress cannot continue indefinitely at the same rate we observed in the 20th century. Jones (2002) extends the analysis of this chapter by relating technological progress to the growth in researchers (scientists and engineers engaged in research and development). In the 20th century, the growth in researchers was based on population growth and on growth in research intensity (the fraction of the available work force devoted to research). Jones points out that the only growth that is sustainable comes from population growth (as with all investment rates, the fraction of the work force devoted to research is bounded). Assuming population growth remains like that of the second half of the 20th century, long-run growth is expected to be less than ½ percent. As is discussed further in Chapter 12, recent evidence suggests (i) research effort is subject to diminishing returns, implying even weaker technological progress going forward, and (ii) government policies are reducing the rates of investment generally.

11. The Growth Miracle begins with independence from Japan that led directly to two important early changes. First, the schooling that was being suppressed by Japanese authorities was now free to take off. Second, there was a land reform that reduced the concentration of land holdings and distributed land more evenly across the rural population. As we have discussed in Chapter 8, these two changes could have been connected. If the country's policies under Japanese rule were largely driven by powerful landlords, then this could have been one of the political forces that blocked the rise in schooling.

Third, the government was eventually controlled by pro-growth dictators that not only invested heavily in public infrastructure but also participated in the formation of large industrial conglomerates. The conglomerates were purposely subjected to fierce competition by opening the borders to international trade. This all sped the formation of private capital, industrialization, and the structural transformation.

12. In the standard growth model from Chapter 2, economic growth rates fall as countries develop. The falling growth rates imply countries with similar fundamentals should tend to the same steady state, with poorer countries growing faster and converging to the living standards of richer countries. In general, cross-country data reveals that countries at different levels of development experience similar growth rates. This is inconsistent with the standard model unless countries at different levels of development have systematically different long-run fundamentals.

In contrast, the growth model of this chapter predicts similar growth rates across a wide range of development even for countries that have the same long-run fundamentals. Thus, a lack of convergence on average is a clear prediction of the model.

13. Africa is an example of a region whose growth may be negatively affected by international trade of goods. Several African countries have a comparative advantage in agricultural goods and primary products. When international markets generate a rise in the relative prices of these goods, resources are reallocated away from modern manufacturing and toward the traditional sector—a reversal of the structural transformation. As a result, growth-promoting mechanisms associated with the structural transformation are weakened.

In addition to the relative price movements from international markets, the structural transformation in Africa has been slowed by domestic forces. These forces include a lack of public infrastructure and related services, high regulatory costs, and low-quality schools.

14. As we have stressed in this text, the timing of the initial modern growth take-off is a key determinant of the relative living standards across countries today. One force delaying the initial take-off is the country's politics.

When a country is undeveloped, it is nevertheless possible for a small fraction of the population to become rich by exploiting the country's available resources and labor. The rich elite are naturally also those that have seized political power. The political power allows the elite to create policies and laws that maintain the status quo and prevent economic competition from anyone outside the small fraction of the population that rules the country. Monarchies, dictators, one-party rulers, overly influential landowners, and traditional craftsmen maintain control by creating monopolies, blocking innovation, arbitrarily seizing land, and taxing income. For our purposes, one can think of this situation as one where the traditional sector of the economy is being protected from competition because most of the income generated there flows to a small group in power and its supporters.

Autocracies are particularly detrimental for growth when the country's population is ethnically diverse. In this case, the tendency of those in power is to control resources for its own ethnic group at the expense of the country as a whole. A particularly bad mix for a developing country is to have an autocratic regime, with an ethnically diverse population, and rich natural resources. Unfortunately, this toxic mix is quite common in developing countries, particularly in Africa and the Middle East. The relatively low current standard of living in these underdeveloped regions is largely the result of a legacy of extractive regimes that have been generated by the combination of autocratic government, ethnic diversity, and natural resources.

Problems

1. This problem involves rewriting the actual relative income from the family business in terms of φ_t and then using (9.8) to solve for φ_t in terms of other variables to get (9.9). Toward this end, write residual income from the family business in terms of the wage bill, as we have done in the past, remembering $\tilde{w}_{t+1}\tilde{D}_{t+1} = w_{t+1}D_{t+1}$ and $\delta = 1$, in order to write the left-hand-side of (9.8) as $\dfrac{\alpha}{1-\alpha} \dfrac{\tilde{w}_{t+1}\tilde{D}_{t+1}f_{t+1}}{r_{t+1}\tilde{w}_t\tilde{D}_t\tilde{z}\tilde{h}_t\varphi_t\tilde{n}_t}$. Now, use the national labor market condition, the factor price equations, and (9.7f) to write this expression out as

$\dfrac{\alpha}{1-\alpha} \dfrac{(1-\alpha)Ak_{t+1}^{\alpha}D_{t+1}}{\alpha Ak_{t+1}^{\alpha-1}(1-\alpha)Ak_t^{\alpha}D_t\tilde{z}\tilde{h}_t} \left[\dfrac{\tilde{a}\tilde{D}_{t+1}}{k_{t+1}^{\alpha}D_{t+1}} \right]^{-1/\alpha} \dfrac{1}{\tilde{D}_{t+1}\varphi_t\tilde{n}_t}$. Next, simplify to get

$\dfrac{1+d}{(1-\alpha)Ak_t^{\alpha}\tilde{z}\tilde{h}_t} \left[\dfrac{\tilde{a}\tilde{D}_{t+1}}{D_{t+1}} \right]^{-1/\alpha} \dfrac{1}{\tilde{D}_{t+1}\varphi_t\tilde{n}_t}$. Finally, plug the expression in for the left-hand-side of (9.8) and solve for φ_t.

2. As discussed in the text and *Problem* 1, the demand for labor from the traditional sector is $\dfrac{\tilde{N}_t}{\varphi_t \tilde{n}_t} f_{t+1} = \dfrac{\tilde{N}_t}{\varphi_t \tilde{n}_t}\left(\tilde{a}\dfrac{\tilde{D}_{t+1}}{D_{t+1}}\right)^{1/\alpha} \dfrac{1}{\tilde{D}_{t+1}k_{t+1}}$. Now, use (9.9) to rewrite the demand as

$$\tilde{N}_t \dfrac{\Omega(1-\alpha)Ak_t^\alpha \tilde{z}\tilde{h}_t}{(1+d)k_{t+1}}.$$

3. Using the results of *Problem* 2, writing out the definition of the capital-labor ratio, we have

$$k_{t+1} = \dfrac{N_t^* \dfrac{\beta}{1+\beta+\psi} w_t D_t h_t + \tilde{N}_t \dfrac{\beta-(1+\psi)\Omega}{1+\beta+\psi} \tilde{w}_t \tilde{D}_t \tilde{z}\tilde{h}_t}{D_{t+1}\left[N_{t+1}^* \dfrac{1+\beta}{1+\beta+\psi} h_{t+1} + \tilde{N}_{t+1} \dfrac{1+\beta-\psi\Omega}{1+\beta+\psi} \tilde{z}\tilde{h}_{t+1} - \tilde{N}_t \dfrac{\Omega w_t \tilde{z}\tilde{h}_t}{(1+d)k_{t+1}}\right]}.$$

Simplifying and solving for k_{t+1} by cross multiplying yields

$$k_{t+1} = \dfrac{(1-\alpha)Ak_t^\alpha \left[N_t^* \dfrac{\beta}{1+\beta+\psi} h_t + \tilde{N}_t \dfrac{\beta-(1+\psi)\Omega}{1+\beta+\psi} \tilde{z}\tilde{h}_t + \tilde{N}_t \Omega \tilde{z}\tilde{h}_t\right]}{(1+d)\left[N_{t+1}^* \dfrac{1+\beta}{1+\beta+\psi} h_{t+1} + \tilde{N}_{t+1} \dfrac{1+\beta-\psi\Omega}{1+\beta+\psi} \tilde{z}\tilde{h}_{t+1}\right]}$$

$$= \dfrac{N_t^* + \tilde{N}_t}{N_{t+1}^* + \tilde{N}_{t+1}} \dfrac{(1-\alpha)Ak_t^\alpha \left[\dfrac{\beta}{1+\beta+\psi} h_t \pi_t + \dfrac{\beta-(1+\psi)\Omega}{1+\beta+\psi} \tilde{z}\tilde{h}_t(1-\pi_t) + \Omega \tilde{z}\tilde{h}_t(1-\pi_t)\right]}{(1+d)\left[\dfrac{1+\beta}{1+\beta+\psi} h_{t+1}\pi_{t+1} + \dfrac{1+\beta-\psi\Omega}{1+\beta+\psi} \tilde{z}\tilde{h}_{t+1}(1-\pi_{t+1})\right]}$$

$$= \dfrac{\left[\bar{\beta}_t + \Omega \tilde{z}\dfrac{\tilde{h}_t}{h_t}(1-\pi_t)\right](1-\alpha)Ak_t^\alpha}{\left(\pi_t n_{t+1} + (1-\pi_t)\tilde{n}_{t+1}\right)(1+d)\dfrac{h_{t+1}}{h_t}\left[\dfrac{1+\beta}{1+\beta+\psi}\pi_{t+1} + \dfrac{1+\beta-\psi\Omega}{1+\beta+\psi} \tilde{z}\dfrac{\tilde{h}_{t+1}}{\tilde{h}_t}(1-\pi_{t+1})\right]}.$$

There are three simplifications that convert (9.12) to (9.13c). First, is the assumption that $\tilde{h}_t = h_t$. Second, use $\tilde{n}_{t+1} = (1+\Omega)n_{t+1}$. Finally, pull out the expression $1+\beta+\psi$ from the numerator and denominator of (9.12) and then combine the remaining terms to simplify as in (9.13c).

First, the structural transformation releases labor from the traditional sector and increases the growth in the modern sector working population. The size of the migration flow depends on how fast the traditional labor supply is growing relative to the traditional sector demand for labor. Faster growth in the traditional sector labor supply lowers capital intensity in the modern sector. For a given supply of labor in the traditional sector, a decline in the traditional sector

A Complete Dual Economy

demand for labor also releases labor that must be absorbed in the modern sector. The migration flow caused by both features causes the modern sector capital intensity to fall.

The negative migration effect of the structural transformation on capital intensity is countered by a second effect that serves to increase capital intensity. Traditional sector households save at lower rates than modern sector households. As households migrate to the modern sector the economy's average saving rate increases and capital intensity rises. Overall, the structural transformation then has an ambiguous effect on physical capital intensity.

4. Equation (9.13c) does not offer an explicit solution for k_{t+1} because on the right-hand-side we have π_{t+1} which is a function of φ_{t+1} (see (9.13b)) and k_{t+1} (see (9.13a)).

5. To derive (9.13e), first note that employment in the traditional sector in period t is $\frac{\tilde{N}_{t-1}}{\varphi_{t-1}\tilde{n}_{t-1}} f_t = \tilde{N}_{t-1} \frac{\Omega(1-\alpha)Ak_{t-1}^{\alpha}\tilde{z}\tilde{h}_{t-1}}{(1+d)k_t}$. Next, write the aggregate supply of human capital as $N_t h_t \left[\frac{1+\beta}{1+\beta+\psi} \pi_t + \frac{1+\beta-\psi\Omega}{1+\beta+\psi} \tilde{z}(1-\pi_t) \right]$. Finally, write $N_t = N_{t-1} n_t \left(\pi_t + (1+\Omega)(1-\pi_t) \right)$. Dividing traditional employment of human capital by the total human capital available to the economy and simplifying yields (9.13e).

The traditional share is clearly decreasing in the fraction of households that choose to reside in the modern sector. Beyond household migration, the share decreases if the demand for traditional labor falls relative to the supply of effective labor.

Chapter 10
Urbanization

Reader's Guide

Section 10.1   Urban Bias

Purpose: The section examines the consequences of an "urban bias," where the government favors the urban sector over the rural sector in the provision of government goods and services.

Sticking Points: (i) The government taxes wages at the same rate across the economy. Any bias takes the form a greater provision of productive government services per person living in cities.

(ii) We assume a migration flow to urban areas, unobstructed by government restrictions. This assumption plays an important role in delivering the main result.

(iii) Another important assumption is that the economy is open to private capital flows. This means migration to the urban sector does not crowd private capital per worker, only public capital per worker.

Take-away: The government favors the urban sector in choosing its allocation mix of public services across cities and the countryside. However, the mix chosen maximizes wages across the economy. Greater public services in the city raise worker productivity in rural areas by encouraging migration and raising the land-labor ratio.

Section 10.2   Growth and Urbanization

Purpose: Urbanization and growth often move together over the course of development. This section discusses the causal relationship underlying the correlation.

Sticking Points: (i) There are several potential drivers of urbanization. According to an "optimistic view," economic growth "pulls" people into the cities. Growth causes urbanization. A "pessimistic view" argues that people move to the city to escape deteriorating conditions in the rural sector stemming from population growth or relatively slow technological progress. Here urbanization is associated with a decline in living standards.

(ii) The optimistic view is supported by balanced technological progress that raises growth and benefits both sectors. The increase in overall wages lowers the relative cost of migration and causes people to move to the city in greater numbers. While some crowding occurs that lowers wages, the direct positive effect of technological progress dominates.

(iii) The pessimistic view is relevant when population growth reduces the productivity of labor in the rural sector and forces people into cities. In this situation, urbanization spreads the decline in productivity and wages across the economy by reducing public good provision per worker.

Take-away: Urbanization is likely the result, rather than a cause, of economic growth (although see section 10.4 for a counterargument). There are scenarios, feared by policy makers, where urbanization can spread a decline labor productivity across the economy.

10.3   Extensions

Purpose: The efficient urban bias result was derived in a simple baseline that captures some, but not all, associated considerations related to urbanization. This section extends the baseline model in three ways to analyze the robustness of the result.

Sticking Points: (i) The first extension recognizes that government good and service expenditure can include consumption goods as well as productive inputs. The key finding is that an urban bias in total government spending raises welfare across sectors for the same reason as in the baseline model—incentives to migrate to the city make households remaining in the rural area better-off.
    (ii) The baseline model assumes a fixed budget for funding government spending. The second extension allows the budget to be an endogenous function of the economy's tax base (income). An endogenous tax base accentuates the efficient urban bias because a greater urban population raises the tax base. This is especially true if taxes are relatively easy to collect in cities.
    (iii) Finally, an urban bias is further justified if government services are generated by a pure or an impure public good. The relative concentration of an urban population near the public good allows more household to benefit from it than in the rural sector where households are more dispersed.

Take-away: The extensions considered do not contradict the logic of an efficient urban bias and in some cases, they strengthen the argument for a bias.

10.4-10.7   Discussion

10.4-10.5   The notion that urbanization does not *cause* growth is controversial. There is some evidence that larger cities, with concentrated production and labor, raise the productivity of individual workers in some way. However, even if these agglomeration effects are real, there continue to be limits to city size. This is certainly true when the city contains a large informal sector or "slums." The slums may be unhealthy environments for small children, which can lower their adult worker productivity.

10.6   Restrictions on migration flows to the city is an urban bias that is not efficient because while it reduces crowding in the city and raises wages there, it lowers worker productivity and wages in the rural sector. Countries fearing urban crowding sometimes place legal restrictions on migration. The Hukou system in China is a famous example.

10.7   There are a few occasions in history when urbanization is reversed, and people start returning to the countryside. This can happen when the productivity of city employment falls relative to that in the rural sector or when health conditions deteriorate in urban areas because of crowding there. We have seen this happen in (i) perhaps the world's first "modern economy," the Netherlands, at the beginning of the Industrial Revolution in England, (ii) the Ottoman Empire, as the relative price of primary products rose relative to manufacturing goods (section 8.2), (iii) the African de-industrialization during the 20th century (section 7.6.1), and (iv) the reverse migration of India during the 21st century as job opportunities in the city have not kept up with population growth, a phenomenon accelerated by the Covid pandemic.

Solutions to Exercises

Questions

1.   At least at the beginning of this chapter we are more particular in thinking of the traditional sector as rural and the modern sector as urban. The fundamental difference between sectors is the technology used in production. The technology used in the rural sector is traditional in that land is combined with labor to produce output, while a modern technology is used in the urban sector where physical capital and labor are combined to produce output. It is important to note that because the same good is produced in each sector, one sector may be viewed as being redundant. In particular, the policy makers favoring the urban sector may choose to ignore the rural sector altogether by failing to provide government services there. In this setting, there is the greatest potential for an extreme urban bias.

2.   The wage gap is not the primary focus of the chapter, so for simplicity we ignore the theory we used in previous chapters that explain large wage gaps based on intergenerational transfers of land and informal technologies. In this chapter we use the more common approach of thinking of wage gaps as being driven by migration costs, which suffices to explain relatively small wage gaps.

Equation (10.13) presents the equilibrium wage gap. Rural wages fall short of urban wages because migration requires a loss of consumption equal to ω_f (transportation costs, goods left behind, a drop in housing quality, and other moving expenses) and a lost fraction of worktime, $\bar{\omega}$, spent in transit and looking for work in city. The lost worktime associated with migration can also be given a Harris-Todaro (1970) interpretation in that those arriving in the city endure a period of search unemployment.

3. To examine the possibility of an "urban bias" in setting policy we allow urban households to determine the allocation of public services across the two sectors of the economy. Given that all urban households in a given age cohort are identical, the choice of government service allocation can be made by a representative household from the cohort of young urban households in each period.

The government budget constraint confronting the representative urban household in making its fiscal choice is given by $G_t + \tilde{G}_t = B_t$, where B_t is the portion of the total government budget that is allocated to fund government services. The representative urban household chooses the allocation of public services to maximize a social welfare function of the form $V_t\left((1-\tau)W_t\right) + \upsilon V_t\left((1-\tau)\tilde{W}_t\right)$, where υ is a nonnegative weight the policymaker places on the welfare of the rural household. To focus on the consequences of an urban bias in politics we assume $0 \leq \upsilon \leq 1$.

4. The solution to the government's allocation problem is $\tilde{g}_t = \dfrac{\mu(1-\alpha)}{\alpha + \mu(1-\alpha)} g_t$,

where we define the de-trended per worker values of $\tilde{G}_t, G_t$, and B_t as lower case values, that is government services per worker in each sector and the budget available per household, all de-trended by the state of technology. Note that the expression is independent of υ, so politics plays no role in determining the allocation of government services across sectors. There is an unambiguous "urban bias" because government services per capita are smaller in the rural sector, but this is purely for efficiency reasons.

The fundamental logic for the efficient urban bias starts with the idea that urban wages are solely a function of urban public services per capita and not the absolute value of labor as in the rural sector where land is an input. This is true because the private capital-labor ratio is independent of migration flows to the city. As the city becomes more populated, the marginal product of capital rises and attracts private capital into the country to maintain interest rates at the world level. This causes the capital-labor ratio to remain constant and thus there is no crowding of *private* capital that would result in lower wages. Also note that the urban wage determines the rural wage when there is migration across sectors. These two features imply that maximizing government services per capita in the city maximizes wages in both locations.

This logic seems to suggest that rural public services should be set to zero. However, to maximize per capita public services in the city, migration must be limited to some extent by offering public services in the rural sector as well. Thus, the sole purpose of rural public service provision is to control urban crowding leading to the maximization of urban public services for a given fiscal budget.

5. The efficient urban bias result depends on the assumption that there is a positive migration flow across sectors. If migration was impossible, or perfectly restricted, then the policy maker's preferences *would* affect the allocation of public services. For example, in the extreme case where the policy maker was only maximizing the preferences of urban households,

the entire government budget would be devoted to urban public services because, with migration restrictions, the crowding effects would no longer be an issue.

More generally, with no migration, υ will influence the size of the bias. For example, if consumers have log preferences the policy solution is $\tilde{g}_t = \dfrac{\upsilon \pi_t}{1-\pi_t} g_t$, where the extent of the bias depends on the relative cost of providing the services, which is a function of the relative size of the urban and rural populations, and on υ.

6. Technological progress raises worker productivity and increases urbanization. The nature of the technological progress is determined by the exogenous pace of technological progress (E_t) and the extent to which the progress is balanced across sectors. Balanced technological progress creates a "pull-factor" that increases urbanization but lowers the intensity of productive government services economy-wide. The direct effect of an increase in E_t raises wages, lowers the relative cost of migrating, and reduces wage inequality. However, because an increase in E_t also lowers g_t, the overall effect on inequality is not obvious. One can show that the indirect effect of a lower g_t, only mediates, rather than completely offsets, the direct effect of a higher E_t.

There is also a "pessimistic" view of urbanization, one revealed by the concerns of politicians who attempt to limit migration to the city. The pessimistic view is supported by the model when the underlying reasons for urbanization are ones that lower the relative productivity in the rural areas and push people toward the city—for example a rise in the rural population or relatively slow technological progress in the rural sector. These factors result in crowding and lower g_t, for any given value of E_t. The reduction in government service intensity lowers wages in both sectors and increases wage inequality. Here, urbanization is associated with falling worker productivity.

7. As discussed in *Question 6*, balanced technological change increases urbanization and does create crowding that reduces government service provision per worker. However, the direct effect of balanced technological progress dominates, and wages rise throughout the economy, even faster in rural areas, reducing wage inequality.

If technological progress is not balanced, and only occurs in the urban sector, a even larger migration to the city is created. In this case, the migration flow can be large enough to create a reduction in government services per worker that more than offsets the rise in technology, causing a decline in urban wages and an increase in wage inequality.

8. A redistributive urban bias can occur when the government is allowed to artificially increase the cost of migration. Increasing the cost of migration, whether directly due to government policy or not, will lessen urban crowding and give rise to an increase in public services across the economy. However, in the rural sector, the effect of rising public services will not be enough to keep wages from falling as fewer workers migrate, resulting in the

crowding of land and lower worker productivity. Thus, the politics of disproportional urban influence in the setting of policy will take the form of raising artificial restrictions on migration or by not taking actions that reduce the costs of migration.

9. With transfers, the basic message of the early analysis carries over; there must be an urban bias and the weight the government places on the rural household has no bearing on the presence of the bias and no direct effect on the size of the bias. The logic for this result is the same as before. The government should attempt to maximize the welfare of the urban household, which indirectly maximizes the welfare of the rural household when there is a positive migration flow. However, some provision to the rural sector is needed to control urban crowding of both productive consumption services and government consumption.

There are some nuances that were not present before. The necessary bias is based on *total* government spending in the urban sector relative to the rural sector. It is now possible that there is no bias in the provision of productive government inputs. Instead, the government may favor the urban sector in terms of consumption good provision and transfer payments.

More precisely, the bias is a constant, in fact the same constant as in the baseline case. The difference is that now the urban policy maker uses consumption goods/transfers to favor the urban households, in addition to possibly providing them with more productive services.

10. With endogenous taxation, the efficient urban bias is stronger than in the baseline case. (i.e. $\tilde{g}_t$ is now a smaller fraction of g_t). The stronger urban bias results from the fact that an increase in $\tilde{g}_t$ carries an additional cost—a smaller tax base and a loss in tax revenue. An increase in $\tilde{g}_t$ raises φ_t and increases the relative size of the rural sector. With a wage gap in favor of the urban sector, an increase in the relative size of the rural sector causes the tax base to shrink. The argument just made would hold even if $\bar{\sigma} = 1$, i.e. even if rural wages were fully taxable. Allowing for a differential ability to collect taxes across sectors further increases the efficient urban bias.

11. With impure public goods, the productivity of the government services depends on the usage of productive capital. For the same population size, public capital in the city will receive greater utilization than in the countryside, because the population is more concentrated in close proximity of the capital. This creates an additional efficiency reason to favor cities in providing public capital that increases the size of the urban bias.

12. Urbanization is much more rapid in today's developing countries than it was in history. The more rapid pace of urbanization is mostly due to two new drivers that were not present in historical development. First, urbanization is driven by demand for urban services in areas where commodities, such as oil, are being extracted and refined. Second, unlike in cities of the past, today's urban population has a fast growth rate apart from rural-to-urban migration. There is relatively high fertility in the slums of urban areas.

In many ways, the poorest areas of cities in today's developing countries look like the traditional sector. Fertility is high, human capital investment is low, and production occurs informally. More so than in studying historical development, one should interpret the traditional sector as one characterized by informal production—whether the location of the production is rural or urban.

If much of today's urbanization does not crowd the infrastructure of the urban elite, because the rural migrants are segmented into slums, then the motivation to provide government services to the traditional sector is weakened.

13. There are concerns that slums create intergenerational poverty traps. One can easily see how this could happen. Moving to the city raises wages and family resources. However, living in the slum is a less healthy environment because of the reduced space and overwhelmed public infrastructure that results in generally unsanitary conditions. Young children in the family are most susceptible to the disease and illness that this environment breeds. Their compromised health has long-term consequences for their adult productivity because of stunted physical development and impaired ability to learn. While the family as a whole has greater resources in the short run, the next generation may be less productive than workers raised in rural areas.

In terms of the allocation of government services across sectors, an intergenerational poverty trap of this type could be ignored by urban elite policy makers. Some aspects of urban crowding, such as crowding of roads and energy provision, lower the productivity of *all* urban workers. However, if the urban elite live a safe distance from the slums, they will not be exposed to the unhealthy environment created by a crowding of health and sanitation services. As a result, the policy makers will underestimate the full cost of migration to the city and the full benefit of basic public services provided to the slums. Even if the goal is to maximize aggregate economic growth, there will be too little public investment in rural areas and the composition of urban public spending will allocate too few resources to the slums.

14. China has had a long history of restricting the internal migration of labor. When the Chinese Communist Party rose to power in 1949, no labor mobility between rural and urban sectors was allowed. Rural to urban migration was formally prevented starting in 1955 by a household registration system, known as "Hukou," that established household residency. Those with urban Hukou were given access to high paying jobs and government services. The advantage of rural Hukou was a claim to land use. During the first 30 years of Communist rule, more than 80 percent of the population remained in rural areas.

As the Chinese economy was reformed and began to grow in the last quarter of the 20th century, migration restrictions were relaxed due to the need for labor in the urban manufacturing sector. However, it has been uncommon for a rural person to be granted a permanent urban Hukou. Recently there has been a movement in China to reduce internal migration restrictions and increase the population flow to cities. The primary motivation for the urbanization push is to increase domestic demand for marketed goods. The urbanization push coincides with a desire to eliminate the Hukou system. This raises difficult questions about how to deal with the land rights of potential rural migrants. In some cases, rural residents are forced off their land or given far below market value for the transfer of land to local government authorities. There have been significant charges of "land grabs" by local officials that benefit from reselling the land at market value.

The pace of urbanization is already rapid in China and will accelerate if migration restrictions are further reduced. The rapid pace of urbanization is one of the reasons that governments feel the need to intervene and control the process. China and India are considering using policy-based incentives to funnel their rural to urban migration into a relatively small number of mega-cities: 10 to 15 cities with average populations of 25 to 30 million people. This is quite controversial because the empirical work mentioned above suggests that the optimal size of city is much smaller. Thus, the formation of mega-cities may create a drag on aggregate growth.

15. The argument that urbanization causes growth comes from microeconomic studies using data from the cities in developed countries. These studies show that the productivity of an individual worker is higher in densely populated areas because of economies of scale, human capital externalities, and information flows.

It is not clear that these features of agglomeration are dominant forces in the cities of developing countries. Developing countries have experienced historically rapid urbanization but their economic growth rates are ordinary on average. This is likely due to the lack of expansion in their manufacturing sector. Today's urbanization in developing countries is associated more with expanding service and informal sectors. Even where the manufacturing sector is expanding, the benefits are mediated by crowding of public infrastructure.

16. McMillan and Rodrik argue that the majority of the Asian-African growth rate difference is due to different responses to international trade. Trade has accelerated the structural transformation toward manufacturing in Asia but slowed it in Africa. In Africa urbanization is mostly due to the rise in "consumption cities" near areas where primary products are produced or due to growth in the urban informal sector. Urbanization is not strongly associated with the structural transformation in Africa.

Problems

1. The population of young urban households in each period, N_t^*, is comprised of the children of last period's urban-sector natives and the young rural households who choose to migrate $N_t^* = nN_{t-1}^* + (1-\varphi_t)n\tilde{N}_{t-1}$. Dividing this expression by N_t, and using the facts that $\pi_t \equiv N_t^*/N_t$ and $N_t = nN_{t-1}$, yields the desired result.

2. First note that $F_t = \tilde{N}_t = \varphi_t n\tilde{N}_{t-1}$. Substitute this expression for F_t into (10.6b) and then solve for φ_t. Next, use (10.2) and (10.5) to write $D_t = g_t^\mu E_t$ and $\tilde{D}_t = (\tilde{g}_t)^\mu (\tilde{E}_t/E_t)^{1-\mu} E_t$ and

substitute into the right-hand-side of your equation for φ_t. Now, arrange terms on the right-hand-side, and use (10.13), to obtain the desired result. Finally, differentiate with respect to $\tilde{g}_t$ and simplify to complete the problem.

3. The government chooses the country's allocation of productive government services to solve the following maximization problem,

$$\text{Max } \{V_t\left((1-\tau)W_t\right)+\upsilon V_t\left((1-\tau)\tilde{W}_t\right)$$

$$+\psi_t\left[b_t - g_t\left(\pi_{t-1}+(1-\varphi_t)(1-\pi_{t-1})\right)-\tilde{g}_t\left(\varphi_t(1-\pi_{t-1})\right)\right]E_t\}$$

where ψ_t is the Lagrange multiplier associated with the fiscal constraint. The government must also account for the equilibrium conditions for urban and rural wages, (10.3b) and (10.13). Substituting (10.3b) and (10.13) in the government's objective function and differentiating with respect to per capita public goods in each sector gives the following first order conditions for maximization

(A1)
$$\left[V_t'\left((1-\tau)W_t\right)+\upsilon V_t'\left((1-\tau)\tilde{W}_t\right)(1-\omega)\right]\mu(1-\alpha)k^\alpha g_t^{\mu-1}E_t =$$
$$\psi_t\left[\pi_{t-1}+(1-\varphi_t)(1-\pi_{t-1})-\frac{\partial\varphi_t}{\partial g_t}(1-\pi_{t-1})(g_t-\tilde{g}_t)\right]$$

(A2) $(g_t - \tilde{g}_t)(1-\pi_{t-1})\dfrac{\partial\varphi_t}{\partial\tilde{g}_t} = \varphi_t(1-\pi_{t-1})$,

and the fiscal budget constraint.

Using the last part of *Problem 2* and (A2) and then solving for $\tilde{g}_t$ produces (10.15).

4. Dividing both sides of (10.13) by W_t gives us a measure of wage inequality,

$\tilde{W}_t / W_t = (1-\bar{\omega}) - \dfrac{\omega_t}{(1-\tau)W_t}$. Balanced economic growth causes urban wages to rise and

increases the ratio of rural to urban wages due to a lower relative cost of migration.

5. Using (10.15), the government budget constraint can be used to write,

$g_t = \left[\dfrac{\alpha + \mu(1-\alpha)}{\alpha \pi_t + \mu(1-\alpha)} \right] b_t$. An increase in urbanization lowers g_t. Combining (10.2) and (10.3b)

gives us, $W_t = (1-\alpha) g_t^\mu E_t k_t^\alpha$. A decrease in g_t, lowers W_t. As revealed in *Problem 4*, a

decrease in W_t, raises wage inequality by causing rural wages to fall faster than urban wages.

6. (a) The urban bias expression now involves the government consumption goods q_{1t} and

$\tilde{q}_{1t}, \dfrac{q_{1t} + g_t}{\tilde{q}_{1t} + \tilde{g}_t} - 1 = \dfrac{\alpha}{\mu(1-\alpha)} \dfrac{\tilde{g}_t}{\tilde{q}_{1t} + \tilde{g}_t}$. The first thing to notice is that the basic message of the

early analysis carries over to this setting; there must be an urban bias and the weight the government places on the rural household has no bearing on the presence of the bias and no direct effect on the size of the bias. The logic for this result is the same as before. The government should attempt to maximize the welfare of the urban household, which indirectly maximizes the welfare of the rural household when there is a positive migration flow. However, some provision to the rural sector is needed to control urban crowding of both productive consumption services and government consumption.

There are some nuances associated that were not present before. First, the necessary bias is based on *total* government spending in the urban sector relative to the rural sector. It is now possible that there is no bias in the provision of productive government inputs. Instead, the government may favor the urban sector in terms of consumption good provision and transfer payments. Second, the *size* of the urban bias is inversely related to the *form* of the provision of goods to the rural sector on the right-hand side. In particular, the greater the fraction of consumption goods provided to the rural sector, the smaller is the urban bias. The higher is v, the higher is the value of $\tilde{q}_{1t}$ compared to $\tilde{g}_t$. Through this avenue the size of the bias may vary with the weight the policy makers place on the rural households. So while the presence of a bias is independent of the weight, the extent of the bias may now vary with the weight.

(b) The urban bias when the tax base is endogenous is

$$\tilde{g}_t = \frac{\mu(1-\alpha)}{\alpha + \mu(1-\alpha)} \left[g_t - \frac{\bar{\eta}\tau}{1-\alpha} \left(\frac{W_t - \bar{\sigma}\tilde{W}_t}{E_t} \right) \right]$$

The efficient urban bias is now stronger (i.e. $\tilde{g}_t$ is now a smaller fraction of g_t). The stronger urban bias results from the fact that an increase in $\tilde{g}_t$ carries an additional cost—a smaller tax base and a loss in tax revenue. An increase in $\tilde{g}_t$ reduces φ_t and increases the relative size of the rural sector. With a wage gap in favor of the urban sector, an increase in the relative size of the rural sector causes the tax base to shrink.

The argument just made would hold even if $\bar{\sigma} = 1$. Allowing for differential ability to collect taxes across sectors further increases the efficient urban bias. In developing countries, it is relatively difficult to tax the traditional sector. The effective tax rate in that sector is less than in the modern urban sector. Assuming that there remains a gap in the pre-tax wages in favor of the urban sector, this adds an additional reason why tax revenue would fall with an increase in $\tilde{g}_t$.

(c) The urban bias with impure public goods is

$$\tilde{G}_t / F_t = \frac{\xi\mu(1-\alpha)}{\alpha + \varepsilon\mu(1-\alpha)} (G_t / M_t)$$

Recalling that $\xi \leq \varepsilon$, the equation indicates that there will always be an observed urban bias in the setting of fiscal policy, $G_t / M_t > \tilde{G}_t / F_t$. In addition to the other features identified under the assumption that government services are private goods, the degree of urban bias also now depends on how advantageous it is to share the impure public goods in the city versus the country—i.e. the lower the value of ξ / ε the larger is the bias.

7. More important than the observed bias, discussed in *Question 6*, is the *effective* bias per worker, $\tilde{g}_t / g_t$, a determinant of the relative TFP in the two sectors. The effective bias is given by

$$\tilde{g}_t = \frac{\xi\mu(1-\alpha)}{\alpha + \varepsilon\mu(1-\alpha)} \frac{F_t^{1-\varepsilon}}{M_t^{1-\xi}} g_t.$$

Note that the effective bias is influenced by the same parameters as the observed bias and, in addition, by the relative population size in the two sectors. We can examine the determinants of the effective bias further by writing out M_t and F_t as

$$\tilde{g}_t = \frac{\xi\mu(1-\alpha)}{\alpha + \varepsilon\mu(1-\alpha)} \frac{[\varphi_t(1-\pi_{t-1})]^{1-\varepsilon}}{[\pi_{t-1} + (1-\varphi_t)(1-\pi_{t-1})]^{1-\xi}} \frac{g_t}{N_t^{\varepsilon-\xi}}.$$

For a given φ_t, a larger country population (N_t) increases the effective bias because of the advantage of sharing impure public goods in the city. Furthermore, one can show that an increase in N_t decreases φ_t as well, generating a further increase in the urban bias. Thus, as the population of the economy grows in size, the economy becomes more urbanized. During this "structural transformation," the *observed* bias remains fixed but the *effective* bias, given above, widens.

Chapter 11
Government Borrowing

Reader's Guide

Section 2.1   Fiscal Accounting

Purpose: Allowing governments to borrow as a way of financing their policies changes the accounting and the economics of fiscal policy dramatically. This section focuses on the accounting changes. Accounting alone can indicate when government borrowing is becoming excessive.

Sticking Points: (i) The important, but somewhat complex, topic of the section is the *government intertemporal budget constraint* (GIBC). This constraint is formed from the single period government budget constraints by solving for newly issued government debt in terms of all other fiscal variables and then substituting the resulting expression for debt payments to bondholders in the next period. By doing this consecutively throughout time, one can collapse all of the (infinite) single-period budget constraints into one intertemporal constraint (see Chapter Appendix A). This is perfectly analogous to how the lifetime budget of a household is formed but here the process extends to the indefinite future (an infinite number of future periods not just one).

(ii) For the GIBC to be satisfied, government debt must not grow at a faster rate than the interest rate. This ensures that the government cannot issue new debt each period that repays the principal and interest on past debt (if the government could do this forever then its spending is not constrained at all). When the GIBC is satisfied, it is true that the initial outstanding debt of the government is exactly equal to the *present value* of future *primary surpluses* (the present value difference between taxes and non-debt expenditures). In this sense the debt of the government is "backed" by future taxes reserved for its repayment.

(iii) A *Fiscal Gap* has arisen in many countries, with the U.S. leading the way, where governments are violating their GIBC. Instead of projected to run future primary surpluses, governments are projected to run *primary deficits* throughout the entire 21st century. Another way of saying this is that the government has massive *unfunded liabilities* promised to citizens (mainly through social insurance programs for retirees) that are not covered by future taxes under current policy.

(iv) There is an empirically relevant situation where governments can get away with not satisfying the GIBC—that is where governments can use new borrowing to payoff old debt and interest. If interest rates are below GDP growth rates, it is possible for the government to use debt in this aggressive manner without seeing an increase in the debt to GDP ratio. In this sense debt can be *sustainable,* stay constant relative to GDP, without satisfying the GIBC.

Takeaways: Low interest rates have allowed advanced countries to aggressively expand debt financing of fiscal policy for several decades without producing large increases in debt to GDP ratios. With interest rates on the rise and economic growth rates falling, it is likely large primary surpluses will again have to be used to stabilize debt to GDP ratios. Developing economies face higher interest rates and relying heavily on debt financing is more difficult for them to sustain.

Section 11.2   Economics of Sustainable Debt

Purpose: In this section we assume that government debt is sustainable and postpone discussing the economic implications of unsustainable debt. The important economic consequences of sustainable levels of borrowing are discussed here.

Sticking Points: (i) When government debt is issued to fund tax cuts, the current generation of workers experience an increase in lifetime wealth if they do not believe that taxes will go back up before they retire. The longer it takes the government to repay past debt (the more they just rollover the debt by issuing new debt to payoff old debt), the more likely it is that current working households will feel wealthier as a result of the policy. This has two consequences: (i) some unrepresented future generations get stuck paying for the tax cut and (ii) national saving decreases, private capital accumulation falls, and economic growth slows. As a result of the policy, future generations both face higher taxes and lower pre-tax wages.

(ii) Due to the way that old-age retirement benefits are financed, they involve an intergenerational transfer like debt financing. Under PAYG financing of retirement, the current generation of workers pays a payroll or wage tax to finance benefits received by the current generation of retirees, a direct intergenerational transfer of income from the young to the old. The payroll tax, and the promise of future benefits during retirement, undermines the savings of the young. The reduction in household saving, reduces capital accumulation and economic growth. Future before-tax wages are lowered as a result, creating an additional burden that younger and future generations must bear to support current retirees.

(iii) Borrowing is more justifiable when used to finance government investment because the rise in public capital generates greater future income that can help to repay the debt. However, using borrowing increases the extent to which government investment projects crowd out private investment. If the goal is to maximize growth, taxes are preferable to borrowing.

Takeaway: Government borrowing that is not repaid relatively quickly, even if sustainable, raises household consumption, lowers national saving, and reduces future income growth. PAYG pension programs have the same negative consequence for growth.

Section 11.3   Political Economy of Borrowing

Purpose: Why do governments rely on debt financing and why has this tendency been on the rise?

Sticking Points: (i) Households favor public debt when they want to borrow but cannot. Households in developing countries with significant financial market imperfections are typically in this situation. A different interpretation of credit constraints is relevant to all countries, including advanced ones. Households may not only want to borrow but may also want their children to repay the debt! This happens when *lifetime*, and not only current, income is insufficient to carry desired spending, including investments in children such as for education and health. When these investments become more important and more costly, the preference for public debt becomes stronger.
    (ii) With slowing worker productivity growth and increasing wage inequality, there is a growing segment of society that experiences an intergenerational credit-constraint and wants the government to borrow to keep lifetime disposable income, income net of taxes and transfers, as high as possible.
    (iii) Political polarization creates incentives to use debt financing as a way of restraining future policies that the current party in power views as unfavorable. Suppose conservatives are in office who want to keep taxes and government spending low. If there is concern that liberals may win the next election and gain control of government, they will be more motivated to carry out large (unpaid for) tax cuts now. This will saddle the future government with more debt burden which limits spending programs. If liberals are currently in office, they will think the same way: carry out large (unpaid for) spending programs now, rack up debt, and make it harder for conservatives to cut taxes if they takeover in the future.

Takeaways: Borrowing constraints and political polarization make it more likely that the public will favor debt financing. Both reasons have become more important in recent decades, explaining the growing tendency to use debt financing.

Section 11.4   Defaults

Purpose: Developing countries are often forced to default on their debt repayments. Recently, public debt has been piling up even in rich countries. When is the repayment of public debt too big a burden? When will a government default on its interest or principal repayment obligations to bondholders?

Sticking Points: (i) Default can be driven by lender expectations. There can be two equilibria, one with default, one without. If lenders *expect* default, they demand higher interest on government debt and this can cause the government to *choose* default (a self-fulling expectation). The higher is public debt, the more likely this outcome is possible.
    (ii) One can jump from a low-interest rate, no-default equilibrium to

Government Borrowing

a high interest rate-default equilibrium just based on a change in lender expectations (a "crisis of confidence").

(iii) When debt becomes a large fraction of GDP, economic growth typically suffers even if no default occurs.

Takeaway: As debt rises relative to GDP, defaults are more common than one might think, especially for developing countries. There have been historical periods where 20 to 40 percent of countries were in default on their public debt repayments.

Section 11.5   Money, Inflation, and Debt

Purpose: This section explains why budget deficits and high inflation rates are strongly correlated, especially in developing countries.

Sticking Points: (i) We have avoided money as an asset throughout the text. Reviewing basic monetary economics from an introductory or immediate macroeconomics textbook might be useful for understanding this section.

(ii) All governments use newly issued money to finance expenditures (known as *seignorage* revenue), but it is typically a small fraction of total revenue sources. It becomes a significant source of revenue when it is difficult to find lenders to purchase newly issued bonds.

(iii) Newly issued bonds become unattractive to lenders when existing debt to GDP ratios are already high. A country that cannot reduce budget deficits have little choice but to use money creation as a substitute for bond financing. In this situation, governments are also tempted to issue money to create unexpected increases in inflation rates that reduce the real value of debt repayment.

Takeaway: In practice, high debt levels lead countries to do one of three things: (i) consolidate fiscal policy and run primary budget surpluses (ii) default on debt obligations or (iii) implicitly default on debt by generating high money growth and unexpectedly high inflation.

Solution to Exercises

Questions

1. The single period government budget constraint is $B_{t+1} = R_{t-1}B_t + PD_t$. On the left-hand side, we have new government debt levels needed to fund spending that exceeds taxes on the right-hand side. Excess spending on the right-hand side includes the repayment of the principal and interest paid to households holding existing debt plus the primary deficit—the difference between all non-debt related government spending and tax revenue.

2. (a) The budget deficit is the change in government debt across two periods—i.e. the new bonds issued to finance the gap between government spending and taxes: transfer payments + government purchases + interest payment on government debt − wage taxes.

(b) The primary deficit is the deficit *excluding* interest payments to holders of previously issued government bonds, so simply transfers + government purchases − wage taxes.

(c) The budget surplus is the government budget deficit times −1. The surplus and the deficit have the same absolute value but opposite signs, the surplus is taxes minus spending.

(d) The primary surplus is government primary deficit times −1. The primary surplus and the primary deficit have the same absolute value but opposite signs.

The deficit and surplus include interest payments as government expenditures. A higher interest rate will raise the deficit and lower the surplus. The primary deficit and primary surplus do NOT include interest payments, so both are unaffected by changes in the interest rate.

3. The *Government Intertemporal Budget Constraint* (GIBC) says the present value of current and future taxes must equal the present value of current and future government transfers and purchases plus the current value of outstanding government debt. It can also be stated as the present value of current and future primary surpluses must equal the value of current outstanding government debt.

The GIBC is a measure of the solvency of fiscal policy—a requirement that the government eventually repays its outstanding debts or, equivalently, that the government services the interest payments on the current debt from taxes if the current debt were rolled over forever (see *Problem* 2). The *fiscal gap* is a measure of the extent to which the GIBC is violated and the government is insolvent. It is the value of the outstanding debt plus the present value of current and future primary budget deficits. If this sum is positive, and not zero, then there is a positive fiscal gap and the GIBC is violated. Violation of the GIBC means the government is attempting to conduct a type of *Ponzi scheme* where new debt is issued to pay old debt and interest indefinitely.

4. Yes, provided that the interest rate on government debt is less than the economic growth rate. In this situation the government could carry out a Ponzi scheme, with new debt paying off old debt and interest, while maintaining a constant debt to GDP ratio as exhibited in Figure 1. It is unlikely that developing economies will be confronted with this possibility. Even when advanced economies find themselves in this situation there are good reasons for them to avoid it. See Mourmouras and Rangazas, *US Economic Policy in the 21st Century* (2023, pp.22-23, 30-35).

5. (a)-(b) Consumption in both periods is increasing in household wealth. The wage tax lowers net wealth and the net transfer raises net wealth, so the wage tax lowers and the net transfer raises consumption in both periods.

(c) The wage tax lowers first period income more than first period consumption, so saving falls. Net transfers raise first period consumption without increasing first period income, so saving falls.

6. Suppose the government cuts the wage tax and finances the loss in revenue by borrowing, Suppose further that the debt issued in period t is repaid in period t+1 by taxing the old in that period to cover the principle and interest. This policy gives the current generation a tax cut. However, the tax cut does not increase the household's wealth because the *same* household is responsible for repaying the debt plus interest in the next period. Wealth and household consumption do not rise, so the full tax cut is used to increase saving by purchasing the newly issued government debt—no "crowding out" of private capital occurs.

Now let's construct a debt policy that crowds out private capital and lowers growth. Suppose, as before, that the government cuts the wage tax and finances the loss in revenue by borrowing. Now, however, suppose the debt repayment is the responsibility not of the current generation but rather the tax burden is placed on some future generation. Under this debt policy, the tax cut raises the wealth and consumption of the current generation. Only a portion of the tax cut is then saved. The increase in saving is smaller than the increase on government borrowing, so household saving used to acquire private capital must decrease. In this case, government borrowing "crowds out" private investment and lowers economic growth. The key difference is that this second debt policy redistributes income from future generations to the current generation and raises its consumption.

7. In a fully funded program, taxes on workers are increased and used to purchase newly issued government debt or, alternatively, to reduce the need to issue new debt. Private savings falls one-for-one with the tax but outstanding public debt is reduced by the same amount—there is no effect on capital accumulation or growth. This policy is the exact opposite of Debt Policy #1 (the first debt policy discussed in the answer to *Question* 6). Neither policy affects capital accumulation or growth.

Under the PAYG pension schemes, the taxes collected from the current period workers are not saved by the government in individual accounts for their retirement or used to reduce the amount of new debt issued to the market. Instead, the taxes are used to pay benefits to retired households in the same period. The higher tax reduces private saving and lowers capital accumulation because there is no offsetting saving by the government on the workers' behalf—i.e. no reduction in outstanding government debt. This policy is similar to Debt Policy #2 from *Question* 6—both policies reduce the funding of private investment and reduce capital accumulation.

Another interpretation is that both policies raise consumption of a generation alive in period t; the young in the case of Debt Policy #2 and the old in the case of PAYG pensions. A rise in the economy's consumption must lower the economy's saving and investment.

8. Taxes crowd out less private investment than government borrowing. Higher taxes cause less saving *and* less consumption. This means private and national saving will fall less than one-for-

one with the tax increase. If the government borrows an equivalent amount of revenue, national saving will fall one-for-one. This result assumes that future generations of workers, and *not* the current generation of workers, face the higher taxes needed to repay the debt. If instead, the current generation was sure that they would face the taxes needed to repay the debt, then all of the tax cut would be saved and the increase in private saving exactly offsets the decrease in public saving, implying no change in national saving and no crowding out.

9. (a) Households are indifferent to the method of financing because using bond financing raises second period taxes by as much in present value as the required first period taxes.

(b) The optimal rule says the return on government investment must equal the opportunity cost of funds, $\mu A g_2^{\mu-1} = 1 + r*$. The government should continue to invest as long as it raises second period productivity and income more than the cost of financing the investment.

(c) The optimal consumption path is given by $c_2/c_1 = \beta(1+r*)$. A higher interest rate lowers the relative cost of consuming in the future, making the optimal consumption path steeper. A higher time discount factor increases the value the household places on future utility gains relative to current utility gains, causing them to raise future consumption relative to current consumption.

10. (a) If households want to *lend* in order to lower first period consumption and raise second period consumption, they would prefer the government use taxes to finance investment. If, instead, households want to *borrow* to raise first period consumption and lower second period consumption, they would prefer the government use bonds to finance investment.

(b)-(c) The government can act as a financial intermediary for the households and generate the same first-best outcomes discussed in parts (b) and (c) from *Question 7*.

11. Government borrowing in international credit markets can raise household welfare when households are credit constrained. The increase in welfare results because the government can borrow on behalf of households who cannot borrow directly.

12. Under the *life-cycle* interpretation, households represent a single generation that lives for two periods. Under the *generational* interpretation, a household/generation lives for only one period. The second period household is a completely distinct generation.

Under the *life-cycle* interpretation, when the first-period household borrows, it also is the household that must repay the debt and interest in the second period. Under the *generational* interpretation, the first-period household/generation borrows and the second-period household/generation is responsible for repaying the principle and interest. Most societies have legal restrictions that prevent parents from leaving debt that their children are required to repay. The restrictions force parents to leave nonnegative bequests only, no negative bequests (generational transfers of financial liabilities) are allowed. The government can circumvent the legal restriction by issuing public debt that future generations must repay.

13. Bequest-constrained households would prefer to borrow to raise consumption and investment and then leave debt to their children to repay. They cannot legally do this on an individual basis. However, if most households face a bequest-constraint, government officials may respond by increasing public debt on their behalf. This relieves the bequest-constraint and makes the current generation of households better-off.

Since the 1970s, the majority of households have seen little or no gain in real income. At the same time, the relative cost of education and health insurance has continually risen. Under these circumstances, borrowing and leaving the debt for future generations to repay becomes increasingly attractive.

14. The combination of polarization and uncertain election outcomes tend to increase reliance on debt financing. The marginal cost of debt is lowered in this environment because (i) polarization means that if the election is lost, discretionary government funds would predominately be used to benefit supporters of the other party and (ii) uncertainty about re-election means there is only *some probability* that the supporters of the current ruling party will receive transfers and suffer a drop in future consumption because of the debt re-payment.

15. Polarization causes uncertainty over future government transfers and private consumption. Public investment increases the future income of *all* types and provides a boost in private income for those who receive no future transfers because their party is not in office. This "insurance" effect creates an incentive to invest beyond the level that is production efficient.

16. Debt repayment requires taxation. Taxing causes a loss of the economy's resources because collecting taxes is costly and because of other "excess burdens" of taxation. If debt repayment obligations are sufficiently high, households are better-off if the government does not repay a portion of the debt in order to limit the necessary tax increase. The extent of the default is limited by the fact that default encourages tax evasion, making any given amount of taxes harder to collect.

17. There are two equilibria, both that satisfy the financial market equilibrium condition, $(1-\theta)R_b = R$. If households expect no default ($\theta=0$) then interest rates will be relatively low, $R_b = R$, the costs of repayment will be low and the government finds it optimal not to default. If households expect default, then interest rates will be relatively high, $R_b = R/(1-\theta)$, the costs of complete repayment will be too high, and the government will find it optimal to default on some portion of the repayment. Which of the two equilibria prevails depends on household expectations about the willingness of the government to repay debt.

18. (a) the higher is b_2, the more costly it is to repay debt, making it more likely that default occurs

(b) the greater the resource cost associated with collecting taxes, the more likely it is that some default is optimal

(c) the more sensitive tax evasion is to default, the less likely default is optimal

(d) if households expect default, interest rates on public debt will be high, making the cost of repaying debt high, increasing the likelihood of default

19. Seignorage is the real revenue raised when the government uses newly issued money to finance expenditures. Money creation causes inflation. Inflation discourages households from holding money as an asset. The less money households want to hold, the higher the current price level and the lower the real revenue the government can generate from the monetary payments.

20. High inflation typically results when the independence of a central bank is compromised by the need to purchase government bonds that are unattractive to other lenders, a transaction that causes new money to enter the economy. As debt becomes high because of persistent budget deficits, this scenario becomes more likely.

Problems

1. Using the product notation we have $\prod_{j=0}^{2} R_j = R_0 \times R_1 \times R_2 =$
$(1+r_1-\delta) \times (1+r_2-\delta) \times (1+r_3-\delta) = (1.2)(1.15)(1.25) = 1.725$.

The present value in period 0 of 100 units of tax revenue received in period 3 is
$\frac{100}{(1.2)(1.15)(1.25)} = 57.97 \approx 58$. If the government were to receive 58 units of extra tax revenue in period 0, they could reduce borrowing and public debt by 58 in period 0. By period 3, the reduction in debt, and the associated interest payments, free up $58(1.2)(1.15)(1.25) = 100$ units of tax revenue that could be used for other spending. Thus, 100 units of tax revenue in period 3 is equivalent to 58 units of tax revenue in period 0.

2. (a) $\frac{1}{R} \sum_{i=0}^{\infty} \left(\frac{1}{R}\right)^i = \frac{1}{R} \frac{1}{1-\frac{1}{R}} = \frac{1}{R} \frac{R}{R-1} = \frac{1}{r-\delta}$

(b) $B_t = \sum_{i=0}^{\infty} \frac{-PD_{t+i}}{\prod_{j=0}^{i} R_{t-1+j}} = (-PD) \sum_{i=0}^{\infty} \frac{1}{R^{i+1}} = \frac{-PD}{R} \sum_{i=0}^{\infty} \frac{1}{R^i} = \frac{-PD}{r-\delta}$. Thus, we have

$(r-\delta)B_t = -PD$, so $0.03 \times 100 = 3$. The government needs to run a primary surplus of 3 over the infinite future to repay its current debt of 100 or, equivalently, to service the interest due if the debt is rolled over forever.

Take-away: Satisfying the GIBC does not necessarily require that outstanding debt be repaid. The GIBC can be satisfied by running primary surpluses that are sufficient to cover the interest payments on an outstanding debt level that is rolled over forever. This is a way of smoothing the burden of debt over all future generations.

3. (a) An increase in the primary deficit causes a parallel upward shift in the transition equation for debt, leading to a higher debt steady state.
    (b) A higher interest rate causes the transition equation to pivot upward from its vertical intercept, creating a steeper slope and a higher steady state debt level.
    (c) A higher economic growth rate does the opposite of (b).

4. The slope of the lifetime budget constraint is not affected because the interest rate is not taxed in the model. The position of the budget constraint is determined by household net wealth, which determines the maximum possible consumption in each period and thus the intercepts of the budget sketch. Taxes and transfers have an ambiguous effect on household net wealth because the wage tax lowers wealth and the net transfers raise wealth. Thus, the budget sketch may shift outward or inward in a parallel fashion.

5. The household's first period budget constraint is $c_{1t} + s_t = (1-\tau_t)w_t D_t$. Using (11.4a) and the first period budget constraint, we can write saving as

$$s_t = (1-\tau_t)w_t D_t - c_{1t} = (1-\tau_t)w_t D_t - \frac{1}{1+\beta}\left((1-\tau_t)w_t D_t + \frac{z_{t+1}}{R_t}\right).$$ Removing the parenthesis and combing terms yields (11.4c).

6. To get (11.4), solve the following constrained optimization problem,

$$\text{Max } \ln c_{1t} + \beta \ln c_{2t+1} \text{ subject to } c_{1t} + \frac{c_{2t+1}}{R_t} = (1-\tau_t)w_t D_t + \frac{z_{t+1}}{R_t},$$ using the procedures in the Technical Appendix.

7. For Debt Policy #1, tax cuts create government debt that is paid back promptly in the next period by reducing z_{t+1}. In this case we have $dz_{t+1} = -R_t db_{t+1} = R_t w_t d\tau_t$.
(a) The gain in disposable first period income, $(1-\tau_t)w_t$, is $-w_t d\tau_t = 100$

(b) The change in generation t lifetime wealth, $(1-\tau_t)w_t + \frac{z_{t+1}}{R_t}$, is

$$-w_t d\tau_t + \frac{dz_{t+1}}{R_t} = 100 + \frac{-R_t 100}{R_t} = 0$$

(c) The change in generation t first period consumption, $c_{1t} = \frac{1}{1+\beta}\left((1-\tau_t)w_t + \frac{z_{t+1}}{R_t}\right)$, is

$\frac{1}{1+\beta}(-w_t d\tau_t + \frac{dz_{t+1}}{R_t}) = \frac{1}{1+\beta}(100 + \frac{-R_t 100}{R_t}) = 0$

(d) The increase in *private* saving, $s_t = (1-\tau_t)w_t - c_{1t}$, is (a) – (c) = 100

(e) The change in *national* saving, $s_t - b_{t+1}$, is (d) – db_{t+1} = 100 – 100 = 0

For Debt Policy #2, tax cuts create government debt that is rolled over and not paid back until some more distant future period, implying that $dz_{t+1} = 0$. Proceeding to trace through the effects as above we now have

(a) $-w_t d\tau_t = 100$

(b) $-w_t d\tau_t + \frac{dz_{t+1}}{R_t} = 100 + \frac{0}{R_t} = 100$

(c) $\frac{1}{1+\beta}(-w_t d\tau_t + \frac{dz_{t+1}}{R_t}) = \frac{1}{1+\beta}(100 + \frac{0}{R_t}) = 66.67$

(d) (a) – (c) = 100 – 66.67 = 33.33

(e) (d) $-db_{t+1}$ = 33.33 – 100 = -66.67

Take-away: Government borrowing that creates debt that is not promptly repaid, raises the wealth of current generations, at the expense of future generations. This reduces national saving and funding for private capital accumulation.

8. (i) *Fully Funded Program*

(a) In the fully funded case, $dz_{t+1} = R_t 100$, so the change in lifetime wealth is

$-100 + \frac{R_t 100}{R_t} = 0$.

(b) With no change in lifetime wealth there is no change in consumption.

(c) Disposable income falls by 100 and there is no change in consumption so private saving falls by 100.

(d) The government uses the tax revenue to buy back, or not issue to begin with, government debt, so $db_{t+1} = -w_t d\tau = -100$ and the change in national saving is zero (drop in private saving exactly equals the gain in public saving or reduction in public dissaving). With no change in national saving, the capital-labor ratio is also unchanged.

(ii) *PAYG Program*

(a) $dz_{t+1} = 100$, so the change in lifetime wealth of a generation-t household is

$$-100 + \frac{100}{R_t} = -100\left(1 - \frac{1}{R_t}\right) = -50.$$

(b) The change in current consumption is $\frac{1}{1+\beta}$ times the change in lifetime wealth or -33.3333

(c) Disposable income falls by 100 and consumption declines by 33.3333 so private saving falls by 66.6667.

(d) The government uses the tax revenue to pay benefits to current retirees, so $db_{t+1} = 0$, and the change in national saving matches the fall in private saving. As a result, the capital-labor ratio also declines by the fall in private saving.

Take-away: PAYG funding of government pensions has several important consequences that are not an issue with fully funded pensions. PAYG funding (1) redistributes wealth to older generations, (2) lowers private saving with no corresponding increase in public saving, resulting in lower national saving and capital accumulation, and (3) subjects the solvency of the program to demographic changes that alter the ratio of taxpayers to retirees

9. (a) First, note that $z_{t+1}/R_t = \tau w_{t+1}/R_t = \tau(1-\alpha)Ak_{t+1}^{\alpha}/\alpha Ak_{t+1}^{\alpha-1} = \frac{\tau(1-\alpha)}{\alpha}k_{t+1}$.

Substituting into (11.7) and solving for k_{t+1} yields the result.

(b) Using the transition equation, the steady state value of k_t is

$$\bar{k} = \left[\frac{\alpha\beta(1-\alpha)(1-\tau)A}{\alpha(1+\beta)+(1-\alpha)\tau}\right]^{\frac{1}{1-\alpha}}.$$ When $\tau = 0$, $\bar{k} = 0.1048$ and when $\tau = 0.15$, $\bar{k} = 0.0624$.

10. (a) Substitute the government budget constraint expression for b_{t+1} into the transition equation for k_{t+1} to get

$$k_{t+1} = \frac{\beta}{1+\beta}(1-\tau_t)w_t D_t + \tau_t w_t D_t - g_{t+1}.$$

$$= \frac{\beta}{1+\beta}w_t D_t + \frac{\tau_t w_t D_t}{1+\beta} - g_{t+1}.$$

With tax financing, $dg_{t+1} = w_t D_t d\tau_t$, $db_{t+1} = 0$, so

$$dk_{t+1} = \frac{w_t D_t d\tau_t}{1+\beta} - dg_{t+1} = -\frac{\beta}{1+\beta}dg_{t+1}.$$

With bond financing, $d\tau_t = 0$, $dg_{t+1} = db_{t+1}$, so

$$dk_{t+1} = -dg_{t+1}$$

(b) First, $\ln(w_{t+1}D_{t+1}) = \ln w_{t+1} + \ln D_{t+1} = \ln\left((1-\alpha)Ak_{t+1}^{\alpha}\right) + \ln\left(g_{t+1}^{\mu}\right)$, yielding the following expression for future wages, $\ln((1-\alpha)A) + \alpha \ln k_{t+1} + \mu \ln g_{t+1}$. Using $\dfrac{d\ln g_{t+1}}{dg_{t+1}} = \dfrac{1}{g_{t+1}}$, $\dfrac{d\ln k_{t+1}}{dg_{t+1}} = \dfrac{1}{k_{t+1}}\dfrac{dk_{t+1}}{dg_{t+1}}$, and the results from part (a), allows one to differentiate the log of future wages and write the resulting expressions in the text under each financing method.

11.

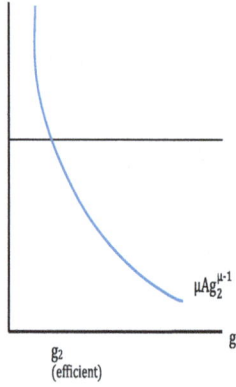

The left-hand-side is a downward sloping function of g_2. The right-hand side is a horizontal line because $1 + r*$ is independent of g_2. The productively efficient value of g_2 is found where the two sketches intersect. An increase in A shifts the downward sloping curve up, increasing the productively efficient g_2. An increase in $1 + r*$ shifts the horizontal line up, decreasing the productively efficient g_2.

12. A lower probability of re-election causes the current government to discount the future more heavily, lowering the effective discount factor. This lowers the expected cost of the lost transfers in the future caused by higher debt repayment. More precisely, the right-hand-side of the first

order condition for public debt will have the coefficient ¼ rather than ½. With a lower expected cost, borrowing will increase in the current period.

13. An even-handed government attaches equal weight to each household type and gives them the same transfers. The government budget constraints are $\tau y_1 - z_1 = g_2 - b_2$ and $\tau y_2 - z_2 = (1+r*)b_2$. Substituting the government budget constraints into the household budget constraints, implies the objective function of the government is then
$\ln(y_1 + b_2 - g_2) + \beta \ln(y_2 - (1+r*)b_2)$ This objective function is of the same form as in section 11.3.1, where the government chooses the efficient investment level.

14. In period 1, the R-type government is in office and the R-type household receives all the transfers, $z_1^R = 2(\tau y_1 + b_2 - g_2)$. Substituting the transfers into the household budget constraint, means the R-type households receive first period welfare equal to $\ln(y_1 + \tau y_1 + 2(b_2 - g_2))$. In the second period, there is a 50 percent probability the R-type government stays in power, in which case the R-type household again receives all transfers, implying second period welfare equal to $\ln(y_2 + \tau y_2 - 2b_2(1+r*))$. There is also a 50 percent probability that the R-type government loses the election, in which case the R-type household receives no transfers and has second period welfare equal to $\ln((1-\tau)y_2) = \ln(1-\tau) + \ln y_2 = \ln(1-\tau) + \mu \ln g_2$.

Putting everything together, the expected lifetime utility of a R-type household is
$\ln c_1^R + \beta E \ln c_2^R = \ln(y_1 + \tau y_1 + 2(b_2 - g_2)) +$
$\beta \left[\frac{1}{2}\ln(y_2 + \tau y_2 - 2b_2(1+r*)) + \frac{1}{2}\ln((1-\tau)y_2)\right]$. The part of the lifetime welfare that a policy maker can impact is $\ln(y_1 + \tau y_1 + 2(b_2 - g_2)) + \beta \left[\frac{1}{2}\ln(y_2 + \tau y_2 - 2b_2(1+r*)) + \frac{1}{2}\mu \ln g_2\right]$.
Maximizing this objective function, by choosing b_2 and g_2, gives the first order conditions stated in section 11.3.3. Equating the right-hand-side of these conditions and doing some algebra yields the expression that implies investment is inefficiently high.

15. The government balances the two costs of tax collection by choosing τ_2 to maximize $\xi \tau_2 y_2 - \frac{\chi}{2}(\tau_2 y_2)^2$. The first order condition is $\xi y_2 - \chi y_2(\tau_2 y_2) = 0$, which implies $\tau_2 y_2 = \xi / \chi$. Substituting the solution into the definition of x and simplifying gives, $x^* = \frac{\xi}{\chi}\left(1 - \frac{\xi}{2}\right)$. Finally, substituting x^* into $\theta = \frac{b_2 R_b - x}{(1-\xi)b_2 R_b}$ and simplifying gives
$\theta^* = \frac{1}{1-\xi}\left(1 - \frac{x^*}{b_2 R_b}\right)$.

16. (a) In a default equilibrium we must have $(1-\theta)R_b = R$ so that the government budget constraint can be written as $x = (1-\theta)R_b b_2 + \xi\theta b_2 R_b = Rb_2 + \xi\theta b_2 R_b > Rb_2$.

(b) Again use $(1-\theta)R_b = R$ to write the government budget constraint as $x^* = (1-\theta)R_b b_2 + \xi\theta b_2 R_b = Rb_2 + \xi b_2(R_b - R) = (1-\xi)Rb_2 + \xi R_b b_2$. So,

$$\frac{x^*}{b_2 R_b} = (1-\xi)\frac{R}{R_b} + \xi < 1.$$ Substituting this expression into $\theta^* = \frac{1}{1-\xi}\left(1 - \frac{x^*}{b_2 R_b}\right)$ gives

$$\theta^* = \frac{1}{1-\xi}\left(1 - (1-\xi)\frac{R}{R_b} - \xi\right) = 1 - \frac{R}{R_b}$$ or $(1-\theta^*)R_b = R$. If $R = 1.05$ and $\theta^* = 0.20$, then

$$R_b = \frac{1.05}{0.80} = 1.3125,$$ implying a default-equilibrium government bond interest rate of 31.15 percent, as opposed to 5 percent in the no-fault equilibrium.

17. In the no-default equilibrium, $x = Rb_2$. In the default-equilibrium, from *Problem 15*, $x^* = Rb_2 + \xi b_2(R_b - R) > Rb_2$. Net taxes, and taxes, are higher with default. Thus, $c_2 = y_2 + Rk + [(1-\theta)R_b b_2 - \tau_2 y_2] = y_2 + R(k + b_2) - \tau_2 y_2$ must be smaller in the default case because $\tau_2 y_2$ is larger.

18. Seignorage is $\dfrac{M_t - M_{t-1}}{P_t} = \dfrac{(1+\mu_t)M_{t-1} - M_{t-1}}{(1+\pi_t)P_{t-1}} = \dfrac{\mu_t}{1+\pi_t}\dfrac{M_{t-1}}{P_{t-1}} = \dfrac{\mu_t}{1+\pi_t}m_{t-1}^d$.

19. Start with $m_t^d = \alpha_1 - \alpha_2 \dfrac{P_{t+1}}{P_t}$. If $\alpha_2 = 0$, then the equilibrium condition for money is $\dfrac{M_t}{P_t} = \alpha_1$. The equilibrium condition implies $\dfrac{M_t}{P_t} / \dfrac{M_{t-1}}{P_{t-1}} = \dfrac{\alpha_1}{\alpha_1} = 1$, or $\dfrac{1+\mu_t}{1+\pi_t} = 1$, implying $\pi_t = \mu_t$. If $\alpha_2 > 0$, $\dfrac{M_t}{P_t} = \alpha_1 - \alpha_2 \dfrac{P_{t+1}}{P_t}$, implying $\dfrac{M_t}{P_t} / \dfrac{M_{t-1}}{P_{t-1}} = \dfrac{1+\mu_t}{1+\pi_t} = \dfrac{\alpha_1 - \alpha_2(1+\pi_{t+1})}{\alpha_1 - \alpha_2(1+\pi_t)}$. For a steady state with constant money growth and inflation, the far right-hand-side term is 1, so $\pi = \mu$.

20. The Bailey Curve is defined by $S_t = \dfrac{\mu}{1+\mu}[\alpha_1 - \alpha_2(1+\mu)] = \dfrac{\mu}{1+\mu}\alpha_1 - \mu\alpha_2$. To find the maximum, differentiate and set the derivative to zero to get $\dfrac{1+\mu-\mu}{(1+\mu)^2}\alpha_1 - \alpha_2 = 0$. Solving first

order condition for the revenue maximizing money growth implies $\alpha_1 = \alpha_2(1+\mu)^2$ and $\mu^* = \sqrt{\dfrac{\alpha_1}{\alpha_2}} - 1$.

21. Substitute the conjectured solution for P_{t+1} into the equilibrium condition for money. One should then get a solution for P_t of the same form (but with different time dating). After the substitution,

$$\frac{M_t}{P_t} = \alpha_1 - \frac{\alpha_2}{\alpha_1} \frac{\sum_{j=0}^{\infty} \left(\frac{\alpha_2}{\alpha_1}\right)^j M_{t+1+j}}{P_t}.$$

Solving for P_t, $M_t = \alpha_1 P_t - \dfrac{\alpha_2}{\alpha_1} \sum_{j=0}^{\infty} \left(\dfrac{\alpha_2}{\alpha_1}\right)^j M_{t+1+j}$ or $P_t = \dfrac{1}{\alpha_1} M_t + \dfrac{1}{\alpha_1} \sum_{j=0}^{\infty} \left(\dfrac{\alpha_2}{\alpha_1}\right)^{j+1} M_{t+1+j}$.

Combining terms yields, $P_t = \dfrac{1}{\alpha_1} \sum_{j=0}^{\infty} \left(\dfrac{\alpha_2}{\alpha_1}\right)^j M_{t+j}$.

SPRINGER NATURE

GPSR Compliance

The European Union's (EU) General Product Safety Regulation (GPSR) is a set of rules that requires consumer products to be safe and our obligations to ensure this.

If you have any concerns about our products, you can contact us on ProductSafety@springernature.com

In case Publisher is established outside the EU, the EU authorized representative is:

Springer Nature Customer Service Center GmbH
Europaplatz 3
69115 Heidelberg, Germany

The manufacturer's authorised representative in the EU is Springer Nature Customer Service Centre GmbH, Europaplatz 3, 69115 Heidelberg, Germany. If you have any concerns regarding our products, please contact ProductSafety@springernature.com

Printed and bound by CPI Group (UK) Ltd, Croydon, CR0 4YY

23/03/2026

02076380-0010